What to Do with Your
Money When Crisis Hits

"If you're one of the tens of millions of Americans who are struggling financially, or if you're faced with helping others who are struggling, you need to read this. Michelle Singletary has written an outstanding book, filled with no-nonsense, let's-get-to-it advice that's immensely practical, easy to read, and emotionally reassuring. Stop lamenting your situation and let Michelle show you the way out of your crisis."

—**Ric Edelman**, #1 *New York Times* bestselling author
of 10 books on personal finance

"Michelle Singletary, a voice of financial reason and calm throughout the pandemic, helps us move forward with what we need most—answers. From when to raid your retirement accounts, go back to school, and so much more, her clear, precise guidance will put you on the right track to rebuild your future."

—**Jean Chatzky**, CEO, HerMoney.com and bestselling author
of *AgeProof: Living Longer Without Running Out of Money or
Breaking a Hip*

"This book is the ultimate first aid kit for your finances. The bandages, the tourniquets, an oxygen tank (if you need it)—it's all here. Every home should have one."

—**Victor Blackwell**, CNN anchor

"This is a compassionate encyclopedia of financial first aid when you stumble, and good financial health practices when you are back on your feet. Michelle Singletary has been the down-to-earth, practical advisor to the stars—and us ordinary folks—for decades."

—**Vicki Robin**, bestselling author of *Your Money or Your Life* and
Blessing the Hands That Feed Us

"This is not only the best book for people facing a personal financial crisis, it's the only book that answers the critical questions you're likely to have. You can depend on Singletary's careful research and compassionate advice to steer you right."

—**Jane Bryant Quinn**, bestselling author of *How to Make Your
Money Last: The Indispensable Financial Guide*

"Michelle Singletary's latest book is full of clear, wise advice that anyone can follow—and everyone should—especially when they are thrown a curve in the game of life. The financial stresses of difficult times can cause paralysis in many people, so Ms. Singletary lays out a plan for dealing calmly with every kind of challenge. My colleagues and I at *Kiplinger's* magazine have long admired the folksy, accessible personal-finance counsel in Ms. Singletary's columns, and here is a big dose of that wisdom in one book. I can't recommend it highly enough."

—**Knight A. Kiplinger**, editor emeritus, *Kiplinger's Personal Finance*

What to Do with
Your Money
When Crisis Hits

What to Do with Your Money When Crisis Hits

A Survival Guide

Michelle Singletary

Mariner Books
Boston   New York

WHAT TO DO WITH YOUR MONEY WHEN CRISIS HITS. Copyright ©
2021 by Michelle Singletary. Afterword copyright © 2022 by Michelle
Singletary. All rights reserved. Printed in the United States of America. No
part of this book may be used or reproduced in any manner whatsoever
without written permission except in the case of brief quotations
embodied in critical articles and reviews. For information, address
HarperCollins Publishers, 195 Broadway, New York, NY 10007.

HarperCollins books may be purchased for educational, business,
or sales promotional use. For information, please email the Special
Markets Department at SPsales@harpercollins.com.

A hardcover edition of this book was published in
2021 by Houghton Mifflin Harcourt

FIRST MARINER PAPERBACK PUBLISHED 2022

Designed by Chrissy Kurpeski

Library of Congress Cataloging-in-Publication Data has been applied for.
ISBN 978-0-358-71921-2

22 23 24 25 LSC 10 9 8 7 6 5 4 3 2 1

I dedicate this book to anyone who has ever fallen on hard economic times, especially those who have suffered because of the COVID-19 pandemic. May you find hope when times seem hopeless.

Contents

Introduction

History has shown us that, however well the economy is doing, we're always only a matter of years away from another recession or another financial crisis that pushes unemployment up and consumer spending down. Inevitably, the stock market will react in a negative direction, erasing gains and causing people to panic. Some may even contemplate moving their money to a savings account that pays a pitiful interest rate.

The 1918 influenza pandemic resulted in 675,000 deaths in the United States. There was also an economic fallout that caused losses for businesses, especially those in the service industry.

Most people know about the Great Depression, which began in 1929 and saw unemployment rise as high as 25 percent. But since then, there have been many other economic downturns that haven't received the same attention or that we've simply forgotten.

The Asian flu pandemic (August 1957–April 1958) coincided with a recession during the same years.

The savings and loan crisis in the 1980s and early 1990s spun the economy into a recession.

During the bull market of the late 1990s, the technology-dominated Nasdaq index soared. But by 2001, the dot-com or tech bubble burst and inflicted a lot of financial pain on people who had invested in Internet-based companies.

The Great Recession, which lasted from December 2007 to June 2009, left many wondering if homeownership was worth the financial risk. It was a brutal time. People lost their homes. Many hardworking Americans bailed from the stock market after experiencing devastating drops in the value of their retirement accounts.

A decade later, in early 2020, the COVID-19 pandemic hit the U.S., eventually causing governments and businesses to shut down. In a matter of just a few months, the fallout caused job losses in the double digits and quickly tanked a historic eleven-year rally in the stock market.

If anything, history has shown us that good financial times don't last forever. So it's not a matter of *if* there will be another recession or economic downturn, but *when*.

WHAT'S IN THIS BOOK

This may sound pessimistic, but I manage my finances as if I'm in a perpetual recession. It's not about being fearful. I'm planning for what I know by now is inevitable. When it comes to your finances, you have to hope for the best but plan for the worst. To do otherwise is to leave yourself unprepared for the next financial crisis, which is sure to come.

During the Great Recession, I fielded a lot of questions from people wondering how to make it through the financial hard times that America was experiencing. A lot of those questions came from people who were trying to make ends meet without having any savings to fall back on. In my experience, these folks were overlooking something important. They weren't taking into account the debt that they'd accumulated and just how much that debt was contributing to their financial insecurity. Debt payments can take you down at least as much as the lack of a savings safety net.

COVID-19 brought a different reason for a recession, but the financial questions were the same as during any other economic downturn.

During tough financial times, our fear drives us to make bad decisions. For example, suppose you have years until retirement but because you get jittery when the stock market drops, you sell your stocks or mutual funds. Sure, you won't experience any further losses, but you've just locked in the losses you've already suffered.

Historically, the stock market has always recovered from hard times. It drops, it hits a low point, then it rises again. If you are no longer invested in the market, you miss out on any new gains. Finally, when stocks have recovered, you jump back in, but by then you're "buying high." That's like waiting for the sale at a department store to end before buying that jacket you've been eyeing. Another example: You notice that people you compare yourself to are buying homes. Because of FOMO (fear of missing out), you rush to buy a home for yourself. Or, you see that mortgage rates are low, and you rush to purchase a home before you're financially ready.

Bad decisions like these can have a lasting impact on your financial life, create financial burdens that can linger for years, cause you unnecessary stress, and limit your choices for your future. The advice in this book is drawn from many years of experience answering questions I've received from hundreds of individuals and couples during in-person conversations, by email, through online forums, at speaking events, and in intensive budget counseling sessions. These people have incomes ranging from nothing at all (that is, unemployed) to six-figure salaries. (Just so you know, your income does not impress me. Your net worth is the true measure of your wealth.)

When I meet with people, I require them to bring a year's worth of banking and credit card account statements. Why? Because people lie to me about their finances — mainly because they lie to themselves first. (*Oh, I don't eat out that much.* Lie!)

We talk about their debts. Often they've separated the debts into "good debts" and "bad debts." The uncommon truth is that there should be just one category — it's all just debt. Debt is a weight that you should aim to drop as soon as you can.

We talk about their saving habits, or lack thereof. Many people can't figure out how to even start saving. It's also important to know how much you should save, and even when it's smart *not* to save. For instance, I'm not impressed that you saved for a year for your wedding when, after the honeymoon, you come home to five-figure or six-figure student loans. That's poor money management. Instead of saving for the wedding, pay off the loans. Then save up for a debt-free wedding celebration. Now that's being money-smart!

The advice in this book might seem harsh, difficult, or impossible at times, mostly because I'm asking you to change how you think about some things. But consider this: Can you really expect your financial situation to improve if you just keep doing the same things that got you where you are in the first place? Or, will you let your fear dictate your decisions? Keep this in mind: You want to be better prepared to handle the next economic downturn than you were when the last one hit. And as I've already said, it's just a matter of time until the next financial crisis arrives.

I'll be asking you to ignore a lot of the conventional financial wisdom that's made us a nation of worried, stressed-out, debt-ridden, panicked people. We need a different perspective on personal finances, one that frees us from the captivity of our own faulty thinking and helps us to sleep better at night.

I've been told by some of the people I've counseled that they often hear my voice inside their heads during trips to the shopping mall or the grocery store or when they are contemplating where to eat out. Others have said they pause before making a purchase and ask themselves, "WWMD" — what would Michelle do? (The *Washington Post* even created a virtual "Michelle bot," a retirement calculator you can find at washington post.com.)

This book includes the most commonly asked questions that I've received over the years as a budget coach, speaker, and syndicated personal finance columnist for the *Washington Post*. You may be familiar with "Frequently Asked Questions" or FAQ pages on websites and apps. I'm adapting that idea to this book, providing an FAQ for your personal finances.

WHAT YOU SHOULDN'T EXPECT

I've learned during my career that I can't possibly answer every question with the specificity needed. After all, no two individuals (or no two couples) will ever be in exactly the same financial situation. (Note: Beware of one-size-fits-all advice. It can be more than just wrong — it can be dangerous!)

With this in mind, think of this book as your invitation to a sit-down question-and-answer session in a room full of people. I can't address any particular question from the group in an in-depth way, covering every aspect of issues raised. However, I can provide you with enough guidance to help you make a better decision or point you toward a resource where you can find the help that you need.

If you're still not quite sure what to expect, you can think of this book like heavy hors d'oeuvres served at a party. They can be filling, but you still may want to eat more later. And you should. I can't cover the universe of personal finance information you need or want to know, but I want to whet your appetite to learn more. To that end, I've included resources — links to websites and calculators I trust, government agencies, consumer groups, and financial institutions — so that you can access the most up-to-date information.

I may not tackle a topic in as much depth as you want, but that's not my goal. The purpose of this book is to provide a starting point of financial advice. Start here, but don't stop here. Make it a new habit to become better informed about your money and the economy so that you can be better prepared when the next crisis hits.

HOW TO USE THIS BOOK

If you feel as if you need answers immediately, then jump to the most pressing questions you have about your financial situation: how to apply for unemployment insurance, whether to save or pay down debt, or what to do if someone asks you for a loan. You might need to know immediately how to manage with less income because you've lost your job. Or, you might fear you're *about* to lose your job, so you need to know if you should temporarily stop investing in your retirement plan. If so, you should get the answer you need right away. But sometimes there are questions you don't even know you need to ask. For example, you might ask if you should rent or buy a home during a recession. But what you should be asking instead is how to reduce your housing expenses. If you're a young adult, this might mean moving back home with your parents. The COVID-19 pandemic pushed millions of Americans, including young adults, to move in with family members, the Pew Research Center reported in 2020. Pew's analysis of census data found that 52 percent of young adults (26.6 million) were living with their parents in the summer following the outbreak of the novel coronavirus in the U.S.

In order to practice sound financial principles that will not just get you through an economic crisis but also prepare you for the next one, you need to build a firm foundation of good decision-making habits, which are the cornerstone of this book.

So, if you can, take time to read all the sections. You'll likely find answers that can prevent dominos from falling in your financial life.

The book is organized into seven sections.

The Basics. This section addresses what to do if you're in dire financial need. I cover topics like applying for unemployment benefits and how to budget when your income drops.

The Past. You can't go back in time and change what you've already done, but if you ask the right questions going forward, you can change your habit of making bad financial decisions. (I'm not judging. All of us have made bad financial decisions in the past. The key is to stop making more of them in the future.)

The Present. What are your most pressing financial issues that just can't wait?

The Future. Yes, you have to live in the present, but you also have to plan for your future needs. In this section, I walk through some of the most frequently asked questions about saving and investing for the future.

The Gig Economy. Maybe you want to work for yourself, or perhaps you've been forced into the gig economy. In either case, you need to have a realistic understanding of how much you can earn, whether your income is taxed, and how to avoid self-employment scams.

The Benefits of Selling Online. Need cash fast? Look for items in your home that you can sell to earn some income. But be careful: Con artists are ready to pounce on your desperation to turn a profit at your expense.

The Schemes and Scams. You need money — like, yesterday. Offers for quick cash seem like just the financial lifeline that you're looking for. But you can make a bad situation awful by falling for offers of fast cash or by jumping into pyramid schemes or other promotions that really make money only for the promoters.

What to Do with Your Money When Crisis Hits

The Basics

What you'll find in this section are the most pressing questions you might have after losing your job or experiencing a decrease in income. Or maybe you're someone who has struggled to budget even when you've had enough money.

If you're financially frustrated, this chapter may be overwhelming. Even so, press through to the end of the section. Some of the advice I offer might be hard to implement. You might not want to follow my suggestions. But come to this with an open mind, and I'm sure that you'll benefit from the advice. I've worked with hundreds of people over the years, and many times I've given comfort to people who are both broke and broken. I'm offering to you what I've offered to them, which are recommendations based on my experience of working with people and watching their situations improve. In most cases, when they listened and applied the advice, not only were these people able to survive, but they also became more financially stable going forward.

WHEN YOU'RE IN DIRE NEED

I've been laid off. What expenses should I pay first?
If there's not enough money coming in, you have to start taking care of your bills the same way a medical staff handles an emergency room full of patients. When staff — or money — is in short supply, you have to use your limited resources strategically. In a process called triage, the emergency-room personnel determine which people get to be seen first by a physician. In this way, the patients with the most critical needs (not just the ones who scream the loudest or are the most annoying) are given the highest priority.

Sticking with the emergency-room example, a patient may arrive at the hospital with a sprained ankle. He waits for an hour, and then a woman comes in and gets taken back for treatment right away. "Wait," the man with the injured ankle protests to the receptionist. "That's not fair. I was here first." But the woman who just arrived is having a heart attack. The man with the sprained ankle deserves care, of course, but he isn't a priority at that moment.

Now back to your money — or lack thereof. There are three categories of triage if you're in a financial crisis: (1) bills and/or debts needing immediate attention, (2) bills that are important and need to be paid but can be deferred or partially paid, and (3) bills that aren't a priority.

If you've lost your job or you're facing a long furlough, you should triage your debt payments and bills, ensuring that the most important bills get paid first.

The first triage category/highest priority: food, gasoline, and child support

You might be surprised not to see rent or your mortgage in this category. But the truth is, if you have a limited amount of money on hand, the most basic necessity comes first, and that's feeding your family. Next comes gas for your car so you have transportation to get the food or to look for a job. If you have children, they are your highest priority and need to be taken care of, even if they aren't living with you.

The second priority: rent, mortgage, auto loan, utilities

Having a roof over your head is vital. However, unless you've been served with a notice to vacate the rental property or there's an imminent foreclosure date, you may have some time before you have to move out of your apartment or house.

If you can't pay your rent or mortgage, the first thing you should do is talk to your landlord or mortgage servicer, which is the company or lender who handles your home loan payments. Explain your situation and ask for assistance. But make no mistake — you *must ask*. Don't hide from the situation by avoiding calls or letters from your landlord or mortgage lender.

You may be thinking, *Why call if I don't have the money?* You might wonder, *What's the point of telling the landlord that I can't pay?*

Communicating may buy you some time. Just let the person or company know the truth about your situation. Be honest about your inability to pay. Ask about your options.

Even if you have a lousy landlord, call. If you've been a good tenant, there's a chance you can work something out. If you've had a great relationship with your landlord, then you are respecting that relationship by telling the truth about your financial predicament. I've talked to a lot of landlords, both individuals and large companies, and they all complain about the lack of communication from their tenants when they get into a financial bind. Keep in mind, your rent is *their* income, and they have bills too. You might still end up with an eviction notice, but at least you tried.

A final word of caution about making your rental payment. The eviction process can be as long as several months in some states, but in others it can take as short as just a few weeks. Make sure you're aware of the laws in your state.

If you have a mortgage, lenders have some leeway in working with homeowners who fall behind. But the longer you wait to communicate about your struggles, the fewer options there may be on the table.

The foreclosure process varies from state to state. It can take as little as six months to as much as several years. In the second quarter of 2020, it was reported that it took an average of 685 days to complete the foreclosure process, according to ATTOM Data Solutions, which collects national property data. ATTOM reported that these states had the longest average foreclosure timelines: Hawaii (1,558 days), Louisiana (1,341 days), New York (1,242 days), New Jersey (1,202 days), and Indiana (1,033 days). The states with the shortest foreclosure timelines were Arkansas (181 days), Minnesota (212 days), Arizona (233 days), West Virginia (254 days), and Michigan (265 days).

Why is the timeline of an eviction or foreclosure important? While having a place to live is vital, if it comes down to making a choice between putting food on the table and paying for the roof over your head, you may have some flexibility in the short term to make the difficult decision to put off paying your rent or mortgage.

Can wait/lowest priority: credit card and medical debt, student loans

I want to be clear about something: Under normal circumstances, you should make every effort to meet all of your financial obligations. However, when you're in the middle of a financial crisis, your credit card payment is most like the patient with the sprained ankle. It can wait. But this doesn't mean you should ignore it.

Contact the credit card issuer to request a pause in your payment. I understand if you're reluctant to reach out to the company. You're stressed, worried, and afraid. The last thing you want to do is explain the obvious again — you're out of work or your income has drastically declined. Still, you need to ask for help. It won't come automatically. You're probably afraid that your request for a pause in your payments will be denied. It might be. However, you won't know if you don't at least reach out to your creditors and ask for some relief. And remember, once you've triaged your bills, don't let creditors on this lower-priority list push you to pay what you can't afford.

Are you worried about your credit score? Don't be. Not now. You can fix damage to your credit history later, after you've recovered financially.

Also, don't let creditors' threats to sue you for nonpayment elevate a particular debt to the top of your priority list.

If you're being sued for a past-due debt, yes, it becomes vital to respond and show up in court. The last thing you want is a court judgment, particularly during a crisis. "If a judgment is entered against you, a debt collector will have stronger tools, like garnishment, to collect the debt," points out the federal Consumer Financial Protection Bureau. "Those tools can include wage or bank account garnishments, as well as putting a lien on your home."

However, even a judgment might not be financially devastating if you're earning minimum or near-minimum wage. That's because a creditor can't leave you so broke that you can't take care of essential expenses. A creditor is limited to taking only 25 percent of a debtor's disposable income (that's what's left over after required deductions such as federal and state taxes). Under federal law, a debtor must be left with an amount equal to thirty times the hourly federal minimum wage.

Here's an example of what this means as explained by the Maryland District Court. Let's say you earn $7.25 per hour (federal minimum wage in 2020). Your gross weekly income (before taxes) is $290.00 (40 hrs. × $7.25). With certain deductions, your disposable earnings equal $232.00. If you apply the thirty-times rule (30 × $7.25), it comes to $217.50. Subtract $217.50 from $232.00 and that comes to $14.50. This is the amount that can be garnished each week. The point is, you have rights as a debtor not to be left destitute. (For more, see the debt collection section at the end of this chapter.)

Once again, keep in mind that if you've lost your job or your income has been cut, it's okay to do what you need to do to pay your necessary expenses. Higher-priority bills should be taken care of before lower-priority financial obligations.

What should I do if I cannot afford to feed myself or my family?

I mentioned before that your top concern should be keeping food on the table. During the Great Recession, millions of Americans applied to the Supplemental Nutrition Assistance Program (SNAP), formerly known as food stamps. It was hard for many people to turn to this program, especially if they had never needed public assistance before that time. During the housing crisis, I counseled a professional who had lost her job with a nonprofit organization. Prior to that she had been making a low six-figure salary. As we sat together trying to figure out which bills to pay, she broke down crying. She shared with me that she had only about a week's worth of food left for her and her two kids. I suggested that she apply for food stamps. "I just can't," she protested. She wanted above all else to be self-sufficient. Eventually, she applied to SNAP. She was approved for only about $50 a month. It wasn't much, but still it brought relief.

Here are a few things you should know about SNAP.

- There are income requirements. But don't assume you don't qualify. If you've lost your job, you may meet the income qualifications. To learn more, go to benefits.gov and search for "SNAP."
- There are special SNAP rules for households with elderly and/or disabled members.
- You must apply in the state where you live. Each state has its own application process.

Make the call. The SNAP toll-free line is 1-800-221-5689. Finally, utilize the food banks in your area. Don't let your pride keep you from accepting food donations. These organizations exist solely for people who are in need, so there's no judgment that comes with your accepting the assistance. You can search for a food bank in your local area by going to feedingamerica.org.

I have a request if you're not in need. If you know a family struggling with food insecurity, which is the inability to provide enough food for their household, give them a grocery store gift card or a general-purpose, preloaded debit card if you're unsure of their preferred supermarket.

What are my options if I can't pay my rent?

Let me repeat this important recommendation again. The first thing you need to do is contact your landlord, and do it as soon as you realize you can't make your next rental payment. You may be surprised at the leniency you might be afforded by staying in communication with your landlord.

If you're receiving federal subsidized housing assistance, contact your local housing authority or your property manager to request that your rent be recalculated if you've lost your job or experienced a loss of income.

Let's walk through some rental relief options.

- Request a payment pause for a month or two. Be aware that a rental payment suspension doesn't absolve you of your ultimate obligation to pay your rental arrears. If you can pull together enough money to pay your rent, do that before asking for rent deferral. The less back rent you owe, the better.
- Ask if you can make a partial payment. Generally

landlords won't accept partial payments. However, during the coronavirus pandemic, many landlords relaxed this rule.

- Ask if you can use any security deposit or last month's rent you may have paid in advance to cover your rent.
- Request that late fees and/or penalties be waived to reduce the amount you'll have to pay once you're able to resume paying rent.
- Contact a nonprofit housing counseling agency for assistance in reviewing your options if you're having trouble paying your rent. Make sure the agency is approved by the U.S. Department of Housing and Urban Development (HUD). For more information, visit HUD's website at hud.gov or call 1-800-569-4287.

One more thing: During better financial times, do your best to be a good tenant. I've been a landlord myself, and I appreciated it when my tenant paid me on time. Because of this, when she lost her job, I didn't press her for the rent or late fees. She was a single parent with a young daughter, and I knew she would pay me if she had the money. I even told her that once she started working again, I wouldn't ask for the back rent or late fees. What would be the point of that? She was so far behind that asking her to catch up would be overwhelming financially. I had enough savings to cover the mortgage.

I will be candid with you. The story still didn't end well for my tenant. I let her off the hook for about three months' worth of rent payments. (It was a small condo, and the mortgage was very affordable.) After the three-month reprieve, she found a part-time job. I asked her to just pay the $100 monthly condo fee. She failed to pay me even that much, so I finally asked her to vacate the property. In the end we parted on good terms, and I was happy to help during her most difficult time because she had been a good tenant before she lost her job.

As a renter, you should take every opportunity to build up goodwill with your landlord so that, when you hit a rough patch, you might get a break. Keep the property in good shape. Make every effort to pay your rent by the actual due date. You may have a grace period, but don't make a habit of using it if you don't need the extra time.

Depending on the situation, your landlord might not be able to afford to give you a grace period. But I recommend that you do what you can to be on good terms with him or her just in case.

My landlord is threatening to lock me out of my apartment. Is that legal?

First, you should understand that your landlord can't lock you out of your rental without a court order. This is not to say that you won't be threatened with an illegal lockout. But your landlord must follow the eviction process mandated in your state.

In 2020, the National Housing Law Project surveyed 100 legal aid and civil rights attorneys in 38 states to determine how tenants were being treated during the pandemic. The survey found that 91 percent of respondents reported illegal evictions in their areas. Tenants were being illegally locked out or faced intimidation from landlords, such as threatening to cut off utilities or refusing to make repairs.

Even if you fall behind in your rent, your landlord cannot retaliate by doing any of the following:

- Prevent access to your unit.
- Change the lock or otherwise lock you out of the apartment or home.
- Remove your belongings from the property.
- Shut off your utilities (water, heat, or electricity).
- Threaten or harass you.

If your landlord is illegally trying to evict you or is using intimidation tactics to get you to move, contact your local courthouse and file a complaint. Get help from a local legal aid organization. Go to the website for the nonprofit Legal Services Corporation (lsc.gov) to find a local legal aid office. Click the link that says "Find Legal Aid." You'll input your zip code and be taken to a page with local legal aid organizations.

At the same time, you should call the police. Be sure to indicate that you are the victim of an illegal eviction. If a responding police officer won't hear you out, ask for a supervisor. You might even be able to file a lawsuit because of the illegal eviction. Nolo.com, a legal website, has a very helpful state statute guide on what you can receive in monetary relief if your landlord takes it upon himself or herself to evict you illegally, which is referred to as a "self-help" eviction. At nolo.com, search for "Consequences of Self-Help Evictions."

If you get an eviction notice, don't ignore it. Go to court and argue your case. Again, get help from a legal aid office near you. The services are free for financially eligible individuals based on income and family size.

Keep fighting to stay in your rental for as long as you can, but you will need a backup plan if all your efforts fail. It is always possible that you might lose your case in court. Be prepared for that possibility by doing your best to find alternative housing before the eviction date. At the very least, pack up the things you really want and will need in preparation for the move.

I've witnessed several evictions and it's a traumatic experience, especially when children are involved. One single mother came home from work to find all of her belongings on the sidewalk. She had three small children. She had been in denial about the eviction and just couldn't accept that it was actually going to happen to her. But, like it has to so many others, it eventually did.

What are my options if I can't pay my mortgage?

The key piece of advice for renters applies to those who have a mortgage: communicate, communicate, communicate. As soon as you know you can't make your mortgage payment, talk to your lender or the company servicing your home loan.

During severe financial times, Congress often passes legislation to help homeowners. And the COVID recession was no different. Under the Coronavirus Aid, Relief, and Economic Security (CARES) Act, homeowners with federally backed mortgages could ask for and receive an initial forbearance of up to 180 days. If additional relief was needed, they were entitled to a 180-day extension. Lenders couldn't levy any late fees or penalties. However, homeowners had to contact their loan servicer to request the forbearance. It's important to note that the forbearance relief was available only to homeowners who had loans owned or backed by the following federal agencies or entities: Fannie Mae, Freddie Mac, the Department of Housing and Urban Development, the Federal Housing Administration, the Department of Agriculture, and the Department of Veterans Affairs. Homeowners with private mortgages were left to negotiate relief on their own. Many lenders, however, did offer forbearance, although they weren't always as generous as lenders covered under the CARES Act.

Mortgage relief legislation was also passed during the Great Recession. In the aftermath of the housing crisis and the resulting surge in foreclosures, the federal government established the Making Home Affordable Program, which included the Home Affordable Modification Program, or HAMP, launched in 2009. Under HAMP, borrowers could apply to have their monthly mortgage payments lowered.

Considering these relief programs, it's reasonable to assume that if another major economic crisis hits, the federal government will step in again to help homeowners. But even if there isn't a federally backed program, here are some mortgage relief strategies that you can initiate by contacting your loan servicer.

- **Request a payment pause.** Ask to forgo paying your mortgage for a month or two. Typically the lender will waive late fees. But that's not always a guarantee.
- **Ask for a payment plan.** Under this relief, you are allowed to spread out your past-due payments, which are added to the regular mortgage amount. Let's say your mortgage costs $2,000 a month and you have been behind for two months. That's a balance owed of $4,000, not including any late fees. But by month three you've started working again. You could negotiate to spread out the arrears. For example, you might pay an extra $200 along with your regular mortgage payment until you catch up. In this case, it would take 20 months of the extra $200 payments to take care of the arrears.
- **Apply for a loan extension.** The past-due mortgage amount is tacked on to the back of the loan, which means

that your loan term would be extended. It also could
result in more interest payments.

- **Modify your loan.** The terms of your loan could possibly
be changed. Your monthly loan payment could be
lowered, for example.

If you don't feel confident in negotiating with your loan
servicer, seek help from a nonprofit HUD-approved housing
counseling agency. One thing is for sure: You won't get mortgage assistance if you don't ask.

Should I ask my friends or family for a loan?

No, don't ask for a loan. Instead ask for *a financial gift.*

Probably the hardest thing about finding yourself in a crisis
is asking for assistance. Or, maybe you've already been a serial
borrower who has burned a lot of bridges. You have a history
of borrowing but never paying the money back, or you don't
stick to the terms you negotiated with your friend or family
member when you asked for the loan. In either case, becoming a borrower beholden to a friend or family member can
ruin a relationship. So ask that the money be a gift, not a loan.
You might say, "I'm in financial trouble and I need help. If you
can afford it, I'm asking you to give me the money, because
I'm just not sure I can pay you back. It's okay if you don't have
it to give, but I would be grateful for the assistance."

If you're like most people, you want the money to come in
the form of a loan, because then you feel you aren't putting the
person out so much. Yet my experience in this area has shown
that many people asking for a loan don't have a realistic idea
of how or when they can pay the money back. They hope they
can, but hope is not a plan.

To avoid an ugly situation down the road, just ask for what you need and don't make any promises to repay. However, if the person you're asking wants the money back, and you have little recourse, here are four rules for being a good borrower.

- **It's the plan, not the promise, that matters.** Your word needs to be backed up with a realistic plan to repay the loan. This is not the time to be optimistic. Be honest with yourself and with the relative about what you can do in terms of repayment. Don't set yourself up for failure. It's better not to rush your repayment plan than to default on the terms of an agreement that's too aggressive.
- **Don't duck and dodge.** If you find you're still struggling and can't honor your payment pledge, 'fess up sooner rather than later. Look, reasonable people understand that situations change and at times get worse. At the start of the novel coronavirus pandemic in the U.S., no one knew how quickly and dramatically it would tank the stock market and the U.S. economy. Jobs that were lost were expected to return rapidly. But that didn't happen. So folks who were furloughed found themselves still unemployed months later or perhaps even permanently laid off. If you can't honor the repayment agreement with your friend or relative, tell that person honestly. Remember the triage analogy? This is the type of obligation that might just have to wait. After all, this is the risk a lender takes, which is why I recommend that individuals should not lend money they can't afford to lose.
- **Put Mama ahead of MasterCard.** When you're back on your feet financially, the bill triage plan needs to be revisited. Personal loans should be given a higher

priority than certain other debts for the key reason that
your relationships are more important than your credit
score. Visa and MasterCard issuers won't come to your
kid's birthday party or to Thanksgiving dinner, nor will
they help you out of a nonfinancial jam like your family
might. Preserve your family ties by making good on your
commitments to them. Or, if you're that concerned about
your credit, ask Mama, the friend, or the relative if it's
okay for her to wait a little longer while you catch up on
the amounts you owe to other creditors. Keep in mind
that it's important to communicate with the people you
owe, especially loved ones.

- **Don't be a trifling borrower.** Nothing makes family
  and friend lenders more furious than a borrower who
  gets an attitude when asked about plans to repay the
  loan. And don't make major purchases to enhance your
  lifestyle while a personal loan goes unpaid. It's incredibly
  selfish to get a new television, take a vacation, or buy
  unnecessary things when you still haven't paid back the
  loan. If you act this way, you'd better hope you never need
  help from family and friends in the future.

What should I do if a friend or family member is in need and asks me for a loan?

I firmly believe that much is required of those to whom much
has been given. So, if someone asks for a loan, offer to give
him or her a gift of cash.

Why? Because most people promise to pay with the best in-
tentions, but then life gets in the way. And when it does and
they can't pay, that's when things start to go bad. Out of em-
barrassment or egotism, the borrower makes up excuses, or,

worse, he starts to ignore your calls. Ultimately your relationship has changed, and not for the better. With this in mind, if you can afford it, just give him what he's asked from you with your blessing and no expectation of anything in return.

Where lending to family is concerned, my husband and I have established a set of rules for granting requests for financial assistance. There are nuances to these rules, so read carefully.

- **What's the reason?** It's important to know why someone is asking for money in the first place. We don't want to give money to support anyone's illegal activities or personal addictions. We also don't want to enable people who continue to make reckless financial choices. (Maybe they've taken vacations year after year with little regard to saving for an emergency.) If the person won't tell us why she needs the assistance, then we won't give her the money.
- **No loans.** We make it clear that any money given is forgiven and never treated as a loan. Even when the person insists on paying us back, no means no. It's important to be genuine about this rule, because if you say it's a gift but you're hoping the person will still pay you back when and if his financial situation improves, your heart will harden if he doesn't.
- **Don't give what you really need back.** Give out of your abundance. I don't care if your mama needs money for her rent. Don't give her your rent money if that's all you have. You may have heard this analogy before, but it's worth pointing out again. Think about the instructions a flight attendant gives before takeoff. Passengers are warned that if the air pressure drops in the cabin and

the oxygen masks drop down, they should put on *their* mask first if they are traveling with a child (or someone acting like a child). When I heard this the first time I flew with my first newborn child, I was like, "No, ma'am, I am taking care of my daughter first." But as the flight attendant explained, you will not be in the position to aid your child if you're gasping for air. "Put your mask on first," we are told. This way of thinking also applies to helping others financially. If you jeopardize your own living situation by giving your mama your rent money, you might need help yourself. Besides, what will Mama do about next month? If she's evicted, perhaps she can come live with you. If she has no way of making her next month's rent payment *and* you lose your job and you can't pay your rent, you're both without a place to stay.

- **A budget is required.** Aside from telling us how the money will be used, the borrower has to show us a personal budget. Yes, this is getting all into *her* business. But the request has to come with transparency. It's not intended to embarrass but to assess if someone is being financially irresponsible. We no longer enable bad financial behavior. We also don't throw good money after bad. I need to explain this last point. If someone is asking for money and it won't really fix the problem but will just kick it down the road, it's better to help her another way. Let's say someone is out of work and being threatened with eviction. There's no way she can afford to stay in the apartment even if you lend her money to pay rent. You may save her for one month, but then she is right back in need the next month. Your money and energy are better spent helping the person find a more affordable or sustainable living situation.

I'd like to share another example of why you should collect more information before becoming a lender. A family member once asked my husband and me to lend her money to pay overdue mortgage payments. But in looking over the person's financial situation, we couldn't see how, after we bailed her out, she was going to be able to pay the mortgage going forward. There was a great possibility that she would still lose her home. So we said no. It was incredibly hard to deny her request and some tears were shed, by her and by me. We wanted to help, yet it would not have been a prudent use of our money. And you know what? It resulted in this person going back to her lender and working with a HUD-approved housing counseling agency to figure out how to keep her home. Our "no" empowered her to work harder to figure out the situation on her own. She ended up asking for a loan modification that saved her home from foreclosure.

Speaking of the housing counseling agency, I direct people to the Department of Housing and Urban Development (HUD). At hud.gov they can search for a nonprofit housing counseling agency that can assist in working with a lender if they find themselves unable to handle their mortgage. On the home page, search for "HUD Approved Housing Counseling Agencies."

- **Make exceptions.** You don't want to enable irresponsible folks, but if someone is in a truly dire situation, that's not the time to wag your finger. Help the person out with groceries or a utility bill. Perhaps your friend or relative hasn't been a great money manager. He has made some bad decisions. But if he has been laid off because of a recession and needs assistance, don't add criticism to an already stressful situation.

Now, if you're going to be hardheaded and ignore my advice to neither a borrower nor a lender be, here are four basic rules to follow.

- **Act like a real banker.** Treat the request as an actual lender might. The bank would review the person's income, expenses, and debt situation to determine ability to repay — and so should you. This can be an awkward conversation, but you need to push through the discomfort and collect some data. Review the person's income and expenses. Ask how he or she plans to pay you back. You should even go so far as to review the person's bank statements. If you're not willing to probe, you're not the right kind of person to be a lender.
- **Evaluate the need.** You're not judging, you're assessing. Sometimes people need to exhaust other options before coming to you for money. I would not lend money to someone who says she is in need but then I see that she has been eating out a lot or shopping for unnecessary things. And yes, you can be the judge of that. You don't want to be an enabler of bad financial management. Why should the person benefit from your savings prowess? Why should someone enjoy the fruits of your frugality when she hasn't stopped her wasteful spending? "I used to lend money to my younger brother," one reader wrote in response to my advice about lending money to a friend or relative. "He rarely paid me back as agreed and often left me struggling to get through the month because he hadn't kept his however well-intended promise. I finally told him I wouldn't lend him any more money. I said if in the future he *really* needed help and I could afford it, I would *give* him the money. He never asked again."

- **Pay creditors directly if possible.** If someone is asking for rental assistance, you should insist that you will forward the payment directly to the landlord. Hard feelings develop quickly when you give money for a specific purpose and the borrower then uses the money for something you did not agree to.
- **Get it in writing.** I know. This rule is hard. Someone is in need and the last thing you want to do is possibly insult her by asking that her promise for the payback be put in writing. Yet crisis situations require clarity. You can purchase a promissory note template at several do-it-yourself online legal sites, including nolo.com and legalzoom.com. You can also find free templates online by searching for "loan agreement." As Benjamin Franklin put it, "Creditors have better memories than debtors."

Are there other ways to find needed funds?

You may have been sent an email or a text from a company or someone claiming he can help you find money you didn't know you were owed. Beware of such pitches. But there is a legitimate way to search for unclaimed money. Unclaimed property laws ensure that financial institutions, other businesses, and government agencies return money owed to consumers.

You can conduct a free search for unclaimed funds on databases run by the nonprofit National Association of Unclaimed Property Administrators (NAUPA), which is a network of the National Association of State Treasurers. Go to unclaimed.org. The databases you'll be searching are located and maintained by each state. Unclaimed property can be money you've forgotten in an old checking or savings account, uncashed check, or a refund. I've heard from people who have found money left by a parent (two sisters found $5,000 left by their father). Another person got back an old apartment security deposit.

You can also search MissingMoney.com. On this site you type in your name and your current state of residence to search nationwide. Of course, to claim the money you must prove your identity.

There are a few other places you can search for forgotten funds. Check out the U.S. Labor Department's "Workers Owed Wages" database at dol.gov. You might find unclaimed retirement plan money at the National Registry of Unclaimed Retirement Benefits (unclaimedretirementbenefits.com).

A LAST RESORT

Should I get a payday loan?

Payday loans are marketed as small, temporary loans. They are popular among people in need because the lending requirements are relatively simple — you just need a bank account and a paycheck. A borrower will either write a post-dated check or authorize the lender to make an electronic withdrawal from his or her bank account. The typical term is about 14 days.

The cost of a payday loan can range from $15 to $30 per $100 borrowed. But when the fees for the loans are calculated on an annualized basis, they can amount to a triple-digit interest rate — from 391 percent to 782 percent for a two-week extension of credit, according to the National Consumer Law Center.

The problem is that a typical customer spends five months

on the payday loan hamster wheel — borrowing more to pay off a previous payday loan, according to findings from the Pew Charitable Trusts.

If you're struggling, you may see a payday loan as a temporary financial fix. You say to yourself that you just need a little more time to get out of a jam. But you should think of a payday loan like a pool flotation device. A typical warning label will caution, "This is not a lifesaving device."

Payday loans give people a false sense of financial security. People think that if they can just make it to the next payday and pay off the loan, they will be okay. But that frequently doesn't happen. Using a payday loan only pushes the problem down the road and often just creates more debt. The repayment costs of a typical loan add up to 36 percent of a borrower's paycheck, according to the Pew Charitable Trusts.

I have always felt that a payday loan is a horrid financial product. Sure, you'll get quick cash, but it can end up drowning you in debt.

I heard I can get money if my car is paid off. So what is a title loan?

With auto title loans, car owners put up their paid-off vehicles as collateral for the loans.

One report by the Consumer Financial Protection Bureau, a federal watchdog agency, found that about one in five borrowers who took out an auto title loan had his car or truck repossessed after he failed to pay off the debt.

Except in states that require lower rates, title loans also carry extraordinarily high rates when the fees are converted to an annual percentage rate, according to Pew. The average car title loan borrower spends about $1,200 in fees annually for loans that average $1,000. "The average lump-sum title loan payment consumes 50 percent of an average borrower's gross monthly income, far more than most borrowers can afford," according to a 2015 Pew report. "The title loan market suffers from the same fundamental problems as the payday loan market, including unaffordable balloon payments, unrealistically short repayment periods, and unnecessarily high prices."

Many people will turn to this type of loan even before exploring other options to find needed cash. In fact, Pew found that most people have other ways to get the money they need. For example, many admitted that they could cut back on basic expenses. "Most also say they could borrow from family and friends, sell or pawn possessions, delay paying some bills, or take a loan from a bank or credit union," the report said.

The Pew report included some complaints from title loan borrowers on how their loans became a trap.

"It's based on an assumption that things are going to get better, and then if they don't you're stuck."
— *Houston borrower*

"It was huge payments that just were out of reach, but I ended up having to borrow to make those payments."
— *St. Louis borrower*

"They took my truck . . . a $2,000 truck, and I borrowed $400." — *Houston borrower*

"They wanted to take my car just for one payment, and I thought that was so very, very unfair. So what I had to do, I had to go to my credit union to borrow the money to pay them back." — *Birmingham borrower*

The problem with this type of loan is that lenders don't look at the borrower's ability to repay. If the borrower defaults, the lender gets clear title to the automobile.

I loathe this financial product just as much as a payday loan. On a list of available money sources to tap if you're in financial trouble, this kind of loan comes in dead last.

When should I tap my retirement money?

Your retirement money should be a last-resort source of cash. But, if you must, it's okay to take from this pot. It's better than taking out a payday or a title loan.

It's easy for experts with fat investment accounts and/or pensions awaiting them when they stop working to chastise you for tapping your retirement fund in desperation. While they are right to caution you, in a crisis you have to do what you need to do to survive in the short term. Sometimes the phrase "It is what it is" rules the day.

If you can borrow from your retirement plan, it should be for high-priority expenses. (Revisit the triage list to remind yourself about how to prioritize your bills.) Not all plans allow loans. Always check your plan for details about what's allowed.

Is it a good idea to take a withdrawal from my Roth IRA?

One source of money — as a last resort — if you find you have no other choice but to tap your retirement funds is a Roth

IRA. A Roth is funded with after-tax dollars, making future withdrawals tax-free.

One of the best features of a Roth IRA is the ability to pull out your contributions without having to incur a tax bill. But there are still some rules you need to be aware of when it comes to using a Roth IRA as your emergency fund.

- You can withdraw your after-tax contributions tax-free and penalty-free any time you want.
- To avoid paying taxes on the earnings and paying a 10 percent early withdrawal penalty, you must have owned the Roth IRA at least five years and be age 59½ or older.
- If you are older than 59½ but don't meet the five-year holding requirement, your earnings will be taxed, but you won't be subject to the 10 percent early withdrawal penalty.
- There are exceptions to the 10 percent early withdrawal penalty (not the taxes on earnings) under some of the following situations: the money is used for a first-time home purchase (up to $10,000) or to pay for unreimbursed medical expenses or health insurance if you're unemployed. You can also avoid the penalty if you're using the funds to cover qualified education expenses or qualified costs related to the birth or adoption of a child.

Should I take out a 401(k) loan or just withdraw the money I need?

If your household has been affected by a crisis, your retirement money may be your last resort. But before you tap this money, consider the consequences.

Let's walk through the pros and cons of a loan versus a distribution.

A 401(k) loan (or loan from a similar workplace retirement plan)

PROS:
- With a loan you won't have to pay taxes on the distribution.
- As you repay the loan, you're actually paying yourself back. Your loan repayments include paying yourself interest.
- Yes, it's a loan, but it's less expensive than racking up charges on a high-interest credit card.
- There's no credit check and thus no ding to your credit score, which happens when you apply for a loan and your credit report is pulled.
- Depending on what your employer's plan allows, you can borrow up to $50,000 or 50 percent of the vested account balance, whichever is less.
- You generally have up to five years to pay back the loan. The loan term could be longer if you're using the money to purchase a principal residence.
- There's no prepayment penalty if you pay the loan back faster.

CONS:
- Money removed from the plan means you could miss out on potential stock market gains until it's paid back. In a down market, you might be okay with this. But in periods when the stock market is soaring, you might be forgoing significant growth.

- If you get fired or laid off or voluntarily leave your job, the loan must be repaid by the time your next federal income tax return is due, even when you file for an extension to submit your return. Prior to the passage of the Tax Cuts and Jobs Act of 2017, borrowers who left their jobs had only 60 days to repay the loan.
- If you can't repay the loan, you'll be taxed on the loan amount, and if you're under 59½, there's a 10 percent early withdrawal penalty. However, if you're 55 or older when you leave your job, you don't have to pay a 10 percent early withdrawal penalty. Check with your company's retirement administration about this rule.
- Some plans don't allow you to make retirement plan contributions while you have an outstanding loan, which also means you could miss out on matching contributions from your employer while the loan is outstanding.

A 401(k) withdrawal or distribution from a similar workplace retirement plan

PROS:
- You don't have to worry about repaying the money.
- It's a source of cash that prevents you from having to borrow money at a time when you can't afford a loan payment.
- It can prevent you from falling behind in your bills.
- If allowed by your employer plan, you may be able to take a hardship withdrawal, but it's limited to the amount necessary to satisfy the financial need, according to the IRS.

CONS:

- You still have to pay ordinary income taxes on the distribution. You need to keep this in mind, because the taxes will cut into the amount you net. The plan administrator is required to withhold a minimum 20 percent of the distribution for federal taxes. Depending on where you live, you might also have to pay state income taxes. Unfortunately, many people don't set aside enough for taxes, so they end up with a tax bill that they can't pay because they've spent all the money.
- Just like with a 401(k) loan, money removed from the plan won't be working for you in the stock market.
- If you're under 59½ there's a 10 percent penalty for early withdrawal. But if you're 55 or older and leave the job, you don't have to pay the 10 percent early withdrawal penalty.

Given the choice, a loan in a dire situation is the better strategy. But if you're not able to take out a loan because your employer doesn't allow it or you're not working, a withdrawal isn't a horrible choice in a crisis.

I've lost my job. Should I take out all my 401(k) money?

Generally, if your account balance exceeds $5,000, the plan administrator must obtain your consent before making a distribution, according to the IRS. Unless you are unhappy with the investment options, you might want to keep the money there, especially if the fees are low. Or you can roll the money over to an IRA. If you aren't in a dire situation, it's best not to cash out and take the money. Yes, you have short-term needs, but remember that this too shall pass and that you will still need to save and invest for your retirement.

Should I keep contributing to my child's 529 plan even though I'm not sure about the security of my job?

If you can, keep making contributions. But if things get really tight, pause the contributions until your financial situation improves. When a crisis hits, move the 529 plan contributions lower on your priority list.

My child is in a private school, but I'm not sure I can afford the tuition anymore. Still, isn't it important to keep that consistency for my child during troubled times?

I have three children of my own. I understand the desire to give them the best. But you can't bankrupt yourself trying to give them more than you can afford.

I've worked with hundreds of individuals through a financial program I created at my church. I've counseled many parents who have spent tens of thousands of dollars sending their children to private school. And, in many cases, the parents' financial sacrifice left them unprepared to weather a job loss or a downturn in the economy.

But before you withdraw your child from the school, talk to the financial aid office. With less income, you may qualify for a tuition break or a grant.

I often ask parents in this predicament, *Did you go to public school?*

The overwhelming majority answer yes.

Then I ask, *How have you fared? Were you able to go to college, get a job? Until the crisis hit, were you living well?*

The overwhelming majority answer, *Of course.*

Even if you live in a school district with a lot of challenges, your child can still get an education. I went to school in Baltimore City, where the school system has had a lot of issues over the years. And still I received a good education. There were many great teachers who made a difference in my life. In fact, in my senior year of public high school, I won a full academic scholarship to college thanks to the support and encouragement of my guidance counselor.

What children need more than private school is financial stability. If you can't get a tuition break, don't break the bank trying to keep your child in a private school that you can no longer afford.

UNEMPLOYMENT

I just lost my job. Do I qualify for unemployment benefits?

Each state has its own guidelines for determining eligibility for unemployment benefits. In general, you qualify if you've lost your job through no fault of your own; are ready, willing, and able to work; and are actively looking for work.

You won't qualify for benefits if you quit your job without good cause. However, go ahead and apply anyway. The only way to know whether you would receive benefits if you left work voluntarily is to apply for them.

Find your state's program by using the "Unemployment Benefits Finder" at careeronestop.org.

I haven't worked in several months. Can I still qualify for unemployment benefits?

When filing for unemployment, you must have earned enough wages during a certain time period to qualify for benefits. A state unemployment agency is going to look at your recent work history to determine the base period. Base periods vary from state to state. If you're unaware of the criteria used for base-period calculations in your state, contact your state's unemployment authorities.

Can I apply for unemployment if I'm self-employed?

After COVID-19 hit the U.S., temporary legislation was passed that allowed states to expand unemployment to people who worked for themselves (independent contractors, sole proprietors, gig workers). But this wasn't a permanent rule.

Absent new legislation, the self-employed are traditionally not eligible for unemployment benefits. Employers contribute to the unemployment insurance fund so that their employees can receive these benefits. Those operating their own business or working as independent contractors don't have an employer paying into the unemployment system so benefits are not available for them.

Can I apply for unemployment benefits if I've been furloughed?

During a financial crisis, an employer may furlough workers with the intention of rehiring them. Under this circumstance, you would generally be eligible for unemployment. However, be aware that if your employer retroactively provides for the payment of your salary, states usually will require repayment

of any unemployment benefits received. Your state will provide you with the information for your repayment options.

By the way, if you worked in multiple states, the state unemployment insurance agency where you currently live should
provide information about how to file a claim with other
states, according to the Labor Department. To find your state
unemployment office, you can go to dol.gov and search for
"State Unemployment Insurance Offices."

Can I get unemployment benefits if I pick up some part-time hours?

In many states you can collect unemployment benefits if you
go back to work but end up working less than full-time hours.
You may qualify for partial benefits. It is important to check
with your state unemployment office on this issue, because
the rules vary from state to state, including how much your
part-time earnings might reduce your unemployment benefits. For example, if you work fewer than four days a week and
earn $504 or less in New York, you may receive partial ben-
efits, according to the New York Department of Labor (based
on 2020 rules). Each day or part of a day you work causes
your weekly benefit to drop by one quarter.

What should I do if my unemployment claim is rejected?

You have the right to appeal a decision to deny you benefits.
And you should appeal.

Many state unemployment systems are outdated, and the
agencies can get overwhelmed with requests for benefits during a crisis. Mistakes happen, and it's possible that you were

wrongly denied. I know it may be overwhelming when you're out of work to have to appeal a rejection of unemployment benefits, but do it anyway. It's your right.

Will my unemployment benefits be taxed?

Yes, unemployment benefits are taxable. In addition to the federal tax, most states tax unemployment benefits. Under federal law, you can elect to have a flat 10 percent withheld from your unemployment check for federal taxes.

It seems unfair to tax already limited benefits. The average beneficiary received just $378 a week in unemployment benefits in 2019, according to the U.S. Labor Department.

Interestingly, unemployment benefits weren't always taxed. Following the passage of the Revenue Act of 1978, unemployment money was taxed depending on the recipient's income. And as part of the Tax Reform Act of 1986, unemployment income became fully taxable.

Why the change? Politicians wanted to discourage people from relying on unemployment benefits. If people made too much from collecting unemployment, they wouldn't look for work, or so the theory went.

That reasoning is idiotic to me and probably to anyone who has been or is currently unemployed. The average unemployment benefits period is about 26 weeks. So why would someone turn down a full-time job for the opportunity to collect unemployment benefits for such a relatively short period?

"If an unemployed worker waits until he is near the end of his eligibility for benefits to consider re-employment, he risks considerable discomfort," one researcher countered in a paper published in the *National Tax Journal* in 1976. "Further,

it has been shown that a spell of unemployment lowers expected subsequent earnings."

Clearly, unemployment benefits are not a permanent so-
lution, so it would be irresponsible for anyone to choose to
turn down a job to collect payments that run out in a fairly
short amount of time. At any rate, you can't refuse to return
to your job because unemployment benefits are higher than
your pay.

HEALTH-CARE COSTS

I don't have employer-provided health insurance.
What's the best option for me to get medical
coverage?

Whatever your political beliefs or party affiliation, can we
agree that our health-care system is leaving too many people
uninsured?

As a general public policy, it seems to me, tying people's access to health care to their place of employment is too tenu-
ous. Lose your job and there goes your lifeline to affordable or
at least financially manageable health-care insurance.

"The health insurance system is a mess," says Carolyn Mc-
Clanahan, a physician turned certified financial planner who
founded the fee-only company Life Planning Partners, based
in Jacksonville, Florida.

In the first half of 2020, 43 percent of working-age adults
did not have stable health insurance coverage, according to
the Commonwealth Fund Biennial Health Insurance Survey. Commonwealth's survey found that one quarter of adults
with employer plans were underinsured, meaning that their
plan had high out-of-pocket costs or deductibles. Many peo-

ple who have health insurance decide not to seek medical attention because of the up-front out-of-pocket expenses. These expenses, not including premiums, can equal 10 percent or more of people's household income, the Commonwealth Fund survey found.

You live in financial fear of a major health crisis when you don't have health insurance.

In 2002, my then eight-year-old daughter developed an unexplained fever. She didn't have a cold or the flu, just a consistent low-grade fever. As it turned out, she had a rare condition that resulted in a two-month hospital stay followed by six months of chemotherapy. At one point during her hospital stay, she needed a spinal tap and surgery to put a central line in her chest because she was getting so much medication.

After a regimen of experimental drugs, she recovered. The total cost of her care came to almost $1 million. If we had not had medical insurance, we would have had to file for bankruptcy, because there was no way my husband and I could have handled that amount of debt. We were fortunate, but so many other families aren't.

Prior to the 2020 spread of the novel coronavirus, nearly six in ten nonelderly people in the United States received their health coverage through their employer or through a family member's job, according to the Kaiser Family Foundation (which, by the way, is a great resource for all things related to health care; see kff.org). As businesses shut down, millions of people lost access to health care.

With every economic crisis or recession, there's the possibility that you too will be looking for health coverage. If this happens, here are some options you may have to consider.

COBRA. At one time if you lost your job, you would be

kicked out of your employer's group health plan. That changed in 1985, with the passage of the Consolidated Omnibus Budget Reconciliation Act, or COBRA.

Under COBRA, you can continue to be covered through your former employer's plan at the group rate. However, this option is available only if you worked for a private-sector company with at least 20 employees or a state and local government. COBRA insurance also covers your dependents. Many states have regulations similar to COBRA to cover employers with fewer than 20 employees, often referred to as mini-COBRA. COBRA does not cover plans sponsored by the federal government or by churches and certain church-related organizations, according to the U.S. Department of Labor. Workers leaving federal employment service are eligible for Temporary Continuation of Coverage (TCC), which is like COBRA. (If you're a federal employee, you can find more information about TCC at opm.gov.)

The downside is that COBRA can be incredibly expensive for many people. In order to keep the coverage, you must pay the full premium, including the share that your employer used to pay, plus a 2 percent administrative fee. For many people, this option is cost-prohibitive.

Also, depending on your circumstances, your COBRA coverage is generally limited to 18 months, although under some conditions the coverage can be extended for up to three years. For more information, go to dol.gov and search for the pamphlet "An Employee's Guide to Health Benefits Under COBRA."

Spouse/parent plan. Under the Health Insurance Portability and Accountability Act (HIPAA), if you or your dependents lose group health coverage eligibility, you may have a right to enroll for different group health coverage without waiting for the next open enrollment season.

With the passage of the Affordable Care Act, or ACA (also known as Obamacare), in 2010, low- to moderate-income families could get financial assistance for health coverage purchased through health insurance marketplaces or exchanges operated by either their state or the federal government. You may be eligible for subsidies or premium tax credits that lower the insurance costs for households with incomes between 100 percent and 400 percent of the federal poverty level. Thanks to the ACA, if you are under 26 you can stay on or rejoin your parents' health insurance plan. At healthcare.gov you'll find a quick guide to the health insurance marketplace and information about qualifying for subsidies.

Medicaid. Under the ACA, states could expand Medicaid to cover nearly all low-income Americans under age 65. All but a dozen states have expanded it to cover people with household incomes below a certain level. Don't assume you can't qualify.

"In states that expanded Medicaid, if income is below 138 percent of the poverty level going forward (about $1,437 per month), Medicaid coverage is an option," McClanahan wrote in a very helpful post with a triage list of how to get health coverage. You can find the article at advisorperspectives.com. Search for "How the New COBRA Rules Affect Health Insurance Planning."

As an aside, Medicaid is not the same as Medicare. People often confuse the two. Medicare is the government's healthcare program for people 65 and older. Certain disabled younger individuals are also eligible for Medicare.

Short-term insurance plans. These plans are meant to be

used temporarily because the coverage is limited. If you're relatively healthy, such a plan might be best if you're between jobs, over 26 and ineligible to be on your parents' insurance, or not yet qualified to sign up for Medicare.

And when I say limited, take that at face value. It's also not likely that such a plan will cover a preexisting condition. You may not be able to get maternity care or prescription drug coverage. Deductibles can be high.

I've lost my job. I can sign up for COBRA, but it's so expensive. What should I do?

The average annual premiums for employer-provided health insurance reached $21,342 for family coverage in 2020, according to the Kaiser Family Foundation. The average annual premium for single coverage was $7,470. On average, workers paid $5,588 for the cost of family coverage and $1,243 for single coverage, with employers paying the rest.

Under COBRA rules, in order to stay covered under your former workplace plan, you have to pay the full premium, including the share that your employer used to cover. So, using the average 2020 figure for family health coverage, you would have to come up with the full $21,342, plus the extra 2 percent, or $426.84, to cover an administration fee.

The question is obvious: How many families can afford a monthly insurance premium of more than $1,800? The answer is, of course, that not many can afford COBRA. If many people are living from paycheck to paycheck and are barely able to afford subsidized coverage from their employer, it's not financially sustainable for them to make COBRA payments out of pocket.

"Leaving your job and losing eligibility for job-based health coverage will trigger a special enrollment opportunity," the Kaiser Family Foundation points out. "You can apply for marketplace health plans and (depending on your income) for premium tax credits and cost sharing reductions during that period. If you enroll in COBRA coverage through your former employer, however, you will need to wait for the next Marketplace Open Enrollment period if you want to switch to a marketplace plan." KFF has a very helpful FAQ webpage that's regularly updated on this issue. Go to kff.org and search for "COBRA."

If you choose to start paying for COBRA, you might find that you can't keep up with the payments. As KFF notes — and don't miss this point — you can drop COBRA and sign up for a marketplace plan and premium tax credits only during open enrollment, which typically runs from November to mid-December in most states.

Don't give up trying to get health-care coverage if COBRA is not affordable. Keep in mind that a major health crisis can make your financial situation worse.

I'm so embarrassed that I can't afford health care. How do I get over this feeling and apply for Medicaid?
There's such an unfair stigma in the U.S. when people have to avail themselves of public benefit programs. But if you need the assistance, apply. This is not the time to let your pride get in the way of seeking the help you need.

How likely am I to qualify for subsidies in the ACA exchange?

About 87 percent of people who were enrolled in exchange plans in 2019 received a subsidy. And the subsidies covered on average 86 percent of premium costs, according to health-insurance.org. The average subsidy was $514 a month, which covered most of the average $594 monthly premium.

When you apply for coverage under the Affordable Care Act, or Obamacare, you may qualify for Medicaid. If not, there are two types of subsidies that can help lower your costs. One subsidy helps pay premiums. The other is a cost-sharing subsidy that can reduce deductibles, coinsurance, and the annual out-of-pocket maximum medical bill cost.

You can shop for plans in different premium price levels: platinum (highest), gold (high), silver (moderate), and bronze (lowest). All the levels offer the same essential benefits. But each level has different out-of-pocket costs. If you opt to get a plan with a lower monthly premium, you'll have higher out-of-pocket costs. On the other hand, if you elect to pay a higher premium, you'll have less out-of-pocket expenses.

Which is best? That depends on what you can afford and the level of care you need. Bronze is best if you need a low-cost plan. This level will cover you for major medical expenses, but deductibles can be high. Silver is a bit better than bronze because deductibles are less. With gold the monthly premium is higher, but more costs are covered. Platinum has the highest premiums, but out-of-pocket costs are very low.

Of course, once you apply for coverage, you'll find out whether you qualify for any subsidies. You can get an estimate now by using the Kaiser Family Foundation Health Insurance Marketplace Calculator. Go to kff.org and search for "subsidy calculator."

Let's say you live in Maryland and your annual 2020 income was $50,000. You are a family of four, with two kids, ten and four. According to the Kaiser subsidy calculator, your income is equal to 194 percent of the poverty level. This means you are probably eligible for assistance through the health insurance marketplace.

How much does a short-term insurance plan cost?

This type of plan — short-term, limited-duration insurance — really is intended to be a stopgap. You might buy this type of insurance if you're between jobs and want to make sure you have some amount of coverage until you can get more. The policies last fewer than 12 months but can be renewed up to 36 months.

Please know that if you have a preexisting condition, you may be turned down for coverage.

Still, as a temporary fix, this might be a viable option. You can find policies for under $100 a month. However, you need to consider the plan's deductibles (the dollar amount you pay before the insurance company starts to pay), copays (the fixed amount you typically pay for a service visit), and coinsurance (the percentage of costs you pay after you've met your deductible).

Please read the fine print of the policy. I know you hear this all the time, and frankly, reading the fine print can be like reading a foreign language. Still, do the best you can to figure out just what you are purchasing and what's not included.

Before considering this kind of policy, visit kff.org (this is my go-to organization for some of the best and most unbiased health-care information out there). Search for "ACA Open

Enrollment: For Consumers Considering Short-Term Policies."

Should I have a health flexible spending account?
What is a health savings account? What's the
difference?

Yes, if you can afford to set aside the money, do it. It's a good
way to shield some of your income from taxes. With a flexible
spending account (FSA), you can set aside money, pretax, to
pay for dependent care or certain qualified health expenses.
You determine how much you want to contribute during your
company's open enrollment period.

Just keep this in mind in deciding whether you should put
money into an FSA. Between 2010 and 2020, the percentage of adults with private insurance who had deductibles of
$1,000 or more increased from 22 percent to 46 percent. You
can spend FSA funds to pay deductibles and copayments but
not insurance premiums.

You can use funds set aside in your FSA to pay for certain
medical and dental expenses for you, your spouse if you're
married, and your dependents. An FSA for dependent care
can be used to cover costs for day care, preschool, before- and
after-school care, and summer camps. The money must be
used for a child under 13, a disabled spouse, or an older child
who cannot care for himself or herself and lives with you for
more than half the year. The maximum dependent-care FSA
contribution for 2021 is $5,000 for individuals or married
couples filing taxes jointly, and $2,500 for a married person
filing separately.

Qualified medical expenses can include copays, deductibles, and over-the-counter medication. In 2021 employees could contribute up to $2,750 to a health FSA, including accounts set up specifically for dental and vision care services.

A health savings account (HSA) allows you to set aside pre-taxed money for qualified medical expenses. You can use this money to pay for deductibles, copayments, or other health-related expenses. You may only contribute to an HSA if you have a High Deductible Health Plan (HDHP). One of the advantages of an HSA is that withdrawals are not taxed, including most state taxes, if used for qualified medical expenses. You can also invest the money in an HSA; however, as with most investments, there is the risk of losing money. Unlike an FSA, which limits the amount of money that can be rolled over into the next year, funds not used in an HSA are yours to keep indefinitely.

If you're in a financial pinch, you may be thinking you can tap the HSA money. If you do, it'll come at a cost. If you take the funds out for a nonqualified medical expense before age 65, you'll owe income tax on the money in addition to a 20 percent penalty. After 65, the 20 percent penalty goes away, but you'll still owe taxes on the money if used for nonqualified expenses. For a list of qualified medical expenses, read IRS Publication 502, Medical and Dental Expenses, which you can view at irs.gov. For information about the tax treatment of HSAs, read IRS Publication 969, Health Savings Accounts and Other Tax-Favored Health Plans.

I'm young and healthy, and I rarely get sick. Can
I cancel my health insurance? I really need the
money!

When money is tight, it's so tempting to eliminate an expense that provides a benefit you aren't using at the moment.
Frankly, it's tone-deaf for experts to chide people when they
skip getting health insurance. If you're looking at the current
need to eat versus the possibility that you'll break your leg
and need medical care, you'll naturally opt to buy food if your
funds don't stretch to do both. So eat. But also do what you
can to put yourself in a position to get a job with health coverage or buy a health-care plan in the ACA marketplace as
quickly as possible. Even a basic policy can save you from ac-
cumulating crushing medical bills.

Consider this from the 2020 Commonwealth Fund health-
care survey. Among adults who reported having medical bills
or debt problems,

- 37 percent said they had used up all their savings to pay
  their bills.
- 47 percent saw their credit score drop because of medical
  debt.
- 26 percent couldn't cover basic necessities such as food,
  heat, or rent.

Half of all U.S. adults worry that a major health crisis
could lead to bankruptcy, according to a 2020 survey by West
Health and Gallup.

If you stay healthy, you can save the money that would go
toward buying health insurance. But if you have an accident
or a medical condition that requires hospitalization or a trip

to the emergency room, you could end up going to see a bank-ruptcy attorney.

If you can't get health insurance, you can't. But comb your budget carefully for any expense that can be reduced, including things you consider to be essential, such as a streaming service, cable TV, and high-cost mobile service. You can't afford to play the hope game, as in you hope you never get sick.

MONEY MANAGEMENT

I don't know how to budget. Where do I start?
First, don't start budgeting by crunching numbers.

I know, you're probably thinking, *What the what?* But hear me out on this. After counseling hundreds of individuals and couples, I've gained something of an experienced insight into the barriers to budgeting, and trust me, it doesn't begin with figuring out how to build a spreadsheet or finding some amazing financial management app. No, drafting a budget begins with a desire and a commitment to have a financial life that isn't always in chaos.

What's the best budgeting tool or software?
The answer to this question is going to surprise you. It really doesn't matter what budgeting tool or software you use.

When people ask me this question, I think about my struggle with losing weight. Throughout my teens and adulthood, even after having three children, I maintained a healthy weight. But then I hit my late forties, and if I ate a peanut, I gained five pounds.

Okay, that's not completely true, but it feels like it.

I tried all kinds of diets, some more successful than others. But you know what I realized? It didn't really matter what diet plan I used. I couldn't control my weight until I decided I really wanted to control my weight.

I'm still working to reach my weight goal, but the journey didn't begin with trying a new diet, but rather with under-standing and accepting that it's not about the diet. It's about my mindset. I had to accept that I was older, my metabolism wasn't the same as it had been, and I needed more sleep. I wasn't as active as I used to be or wanted to be. My life had shifted and my eating and exercising habits hadn't. Would spending money on home gym equipment make me skinny again? Not if I used the treadmill to drape my clothes.

The same thing applies to budgeting tools. It's your mo-tivation that makes the tool work, not the clever features of the budget software. For most people, budgeting begins with shifting your attitudes and behaviors. How badly do you hate having more month than money? In other words, you're broke by the end of the month, and deep down you know it doesn't have to be that way.

You're probably struggling with your budget not because you haven't downloaded a budgeting app but because you've made decisions to obligate your income for those things you don't really need and can't afford. Sure, you need a car to get to work. But did it have to be a $40,000 vehicle? Or did you buy a car outside your budget range because you "had" to have a certain make and model?

My grandmother Big Mama, whom I went to live with at the age of four, used to budget on the back of junk-mail enve-lopes. She always used a pencil. She'd write down her net pay — what she brought home after taxes — and then list all her bills. If things weren't adding up, she'd start erasing. She'd cut her expenses to make ends meet.

What I admired about her the most was that she didn't feel bad about going without certain things. My grandmother never apologized for what she couldn't buy me or my four siblings, whom she also took in and cared for. Big Mama didn't earn a lot of money as a nursing assistant, but she lived within her means – on a budget – by actively deciding it was the only way to live.

Sure, you can use Mint.com, or a Quicken product, You Need a Budget (YNAB), or Mvelopes, or whatever latest cool mobile budgeting app is popular in the Apple, Google, or Android store. Online or mobile budgeting tools can make it easier for you to track your spending or set up savings goals. Apps often have appealing features, like the ability to sync with your bank accounts, alert you to billing due dates, and remind you to save.

But once you decide that you want to reduce the weight you feel from money worries, any method will do, even just pencil and paper. The tool is just that – a tool, an assistant.

Really, what's the point of a budget when I'm broke?

It can seem ridiculous to suggest that someone stick to a budget when she has lost a job or is living from paycheck to paycheck. Nonetheless, budgeting is about having a command over your money, regardless of the amount. Being broke doesn't mean you give up. Manage what you have, even when it's a little.

The way I look at it, budgeting is like using a GPS app. You can be following a map closely and still take a wrong turn. When this happens you don't just pull the car over and park and throw up your hands in defeat, right? The app redirects you, and you take the alternative route. Or, you make a simple U-turn. A budget can become your financial GPS.

If your money is tight, look at your numbers to see what you can do to reroute your finances. Perhaps you've already cut expenses. Well, maybe you can cut some more. Perhaps you need to move, get a roommate, take on a second job, or ask for help.

Let the budget guide you to where you want to be financially.

How can I stay on track with my budget?

I've already described how a budget can help you find your way out of financial hard times. But there's more that a budget can do for you. One word keeps me on track for my budget: goals. Ask yourself right now, *What do I really want to accomplish with the money I earn?* Then tell yourself the answer.

Over the years I have told myself that

- I want to retire before I need a walker or wheelchair.
- I want to send all my kids to college with no debt.
- I want to pay off my home mortgage before I retire. (If housing is your largest expense, how sweet would it be to get rid of that mortgage and use those funds for fun things, like more traveling?)
- I want to be able to take long vacations — not just for a week or two. I want to sit at the ocean's edge. My most peaceful place is sitting on a beach and simply listening to the tide come in and go out.
- I want to have the resources to help family members go

to college or assist my children with purchasing their first home.

It's those desires that drive me to stick to my budget.

What are your financial goals? Think beyond your current situation and consider the question carefully. Then make a promise to yourself to go after your goals. Once you do that, it's much easier to stay on track.

How often should I revisit my budget?

Your budget isn't something you create and then set aside. Revisit it as often as needed to ensure that you are living within your means. Rework it if a crisis hits, or when more money is coming in and you have an opportunity to save more or pay off debt.

While you're first getting the hang of budgeting, look at your budget often. Become intimate with your numbers. Get to know how your expenses cut into your income each month. Don't just set it and forget it. Remember, your budget is your buddy!

How much should I be spending on major expense items in my budget, such as housing?

The U.S. Bureau of Labor Statistics's Consumer Expenditure Survey is a good guideline to determine if you are out of line in your spending compared to other Americans. Use the average expenditures on major items for 2019 as a guideline:

Housing: 32.8 percent
Transportation: 17 percent

Food: 12.9 percent
Personal insurance and pensions: 11.4 percent
Health care: 8.2 percent
Apparel and services: 3 percent

For example, if you were to keep your housing costs to about 33 percent, those costs would be $1,100 a month on a net annual income of $40,000. I know this may be hard if you live in a high-cost area. However, when your housing costs start to reach 40 percent or 50 percent of your income (and please calculate it on a net basis, meaning after taxes), it's going to be difficult for you to save for life's unexpected financial emergencies.

Don't go by what the mortgage lenders say you can afford. They use your gross income to determine how much to lend you after taking into account your debts. I have just one question for you: Do you bring home your gross pay? No, I didn't think so.

In general, if you find that you're spending more of your net income than the recommended percentages, then these are good places to start if you need to trim your expenses.

I just hate budgeting. It's so negative. Why do I need a budget to tell me what I can't do?
Well, if you like being broke, then don't budget.

You may have heard that budgeting doesn't matter because most people don't do it anyway. Or you might feel that a budget is too restrictive, telling you what you can't do. And sure, that's aggravating.

However, I don't think *budget* is a bad word. I actually love budgeting. I have two loves in my life — my budget and my

"Boo," my husband. Having an intimate relationship with my numbers makes me care more about how those dollars are spent. A budget tells me what I can do. It directs me toward my values and goals.

If you want to become wealthy, you need to get a handle on what's coming in and what's going out. It's only in capturing the extra money you have that you can then put it to work for you. If you're like me, you want to have your money working for you rather than you working until your dying day.

SAVINGS

How much do I really need to save in an emergency fund?

Actually, I believe you need two types of rainy-day funds, an emergency fund and a "life happens" fund. Here's where they differ:

Emergency fund. This is a pot of money you tap into if you lose your job or perhaps get sick and run out of sick leave. It's your income replacement account.

Aim to have three to six months of living expenses in your emergency fund. Include all your monthly expenses—housing, transportation, utilities, cable, streaming services, insurance, etc. It's not enough to just save for your rent and car payment. When people have a disruption in their income, I often find that it takes a few months before they start to seriously reduce their expenses.

So, if it costs $3,000 to run your household on a monthly basis, you should aim to save $9,000 in order to have at least three months of expenses. Don't let that figure scare you. If you can only manage to save one month's worth of living expenses, that's fine. It's a start.

If you are a highly compensated individual or an older worker, set a goal to save six months' to a year's worth of living expenses. During the Great Recession, nearly half of unemployed adults aged 25 to 34 found a job within six months, according to a 2012 brief by the Urban Institute. It took seven months for people aged 35 to 49, and for unemployed adults 50 to 61, the job search took more than nine months. The situation was more dire for adults 62 and older. Only about a third found work within 12 months, and only 41 percent of older workers were reemployed within 18 months. Many just gave up and chose to start collecting Social Security.

"Life happens" fund. This is for those things in life that happen—your car needs repair, your kid breaks the dishwasher. If you own a home, you keep money stashed in this account for home repairs and renovations. This is the account where it's okay for money to come and go. It's there to keep the emergency fund from being drained.

Initially set a goal of saving $500 to $1,000. Eventually you'll want the account to hold enough funds to pay for a major expense without having to put it on a credit card.

Let me add this about the issue of having an emergency fund. Some people get annoyed at the constant reminder to save. They argue that the advice is insensitive when so many people are living from paycheck to paycheck.

"With everything we have to pay for, we just don't need to be condescended to," pushed back one reader of my *Washington Post* column when I implored people to save. "People do their best. If we were able to save, we would."

It's true that many people are struggling, and the recommendation that they should amass three months' worth of living expenses is unattainable. But so many others—you, perhaps—could save more. Believe it or not, you do have room in your budget to create a cushion for when life happens. And somehow it always does.

"We are all guilty of replacing logic with emotion at the checkout counter," another reader added. "It does not matter what you earn. I had a furniture store guy tell me I would be shocked at the number of high-income people who could not get financed for a new room of furniture. He said he had a lady making 40 grand a month get turned down."

Someone else wrote, "The number of families who have taken their kids to Disney World (sometimes numerous times) yet couldn't pull together $500 for an emergency bill just stuns me."

You may be among the cynics who think there's still no need to tell people to save. "I guess there is nothing wrong with friendly reminders, but come on, 'save for a rainy day' is not exactly new advice," another person wrote.

Think of these repeated reminders of the need to save to be something like a fire drill. Of course it annoys you when the siren goes off, but in a panic people don't think straight. Hearing a fire alarm and then practicing what you should do before a fire actually breaks out can save your life. The same is true for the repeated advice to save. The advice is still necessary. The Federal Reserve says many households couldn't handle a $400 emergency without first having to sell something or borrow money from friends or relatives.

You have to be prepared. We need fire drills because, when there are no fires, we become complacent. When times are good, people tend to overspend, failing to prepare for a financial fire.

So yes, the advice to save as much as you can is necessary. It never gets old.

Where should I keep my emergency funds?

I suggest you keep your emergency and "life happens" funds in a bank or credit union. If you want to earn a little more interest, you can look for an FDIC-insured online institution. Check out Bankrate.com for institutions offering the highest interest rates for deposit accounts.

Get a debit card for the accounts, but don't keep it in your wallet. Tuck it away in a safe place. You don't want to make it too easy to tap those funds.

Why shouldn't I invest my emergency money?

Your emergency fund should stay liquid so it's easily accessible if you need it.

My grandmother Big Mama used to say, "Every penny ought to have a purpose." Your emergency and "life happens" funds aren't meant to grow. The purpose of these pots of money is to guarantee that the money is there if a financial emergency comes up. You should not risk any money you need, even if you aren't sure when you'll need it.

What if you have a financial emergency just as there's a significant downturn in the stock market? You don't want to be forced to sell and take a loss. The general rule is, don't invest money you may need within a five-year period.

Remember: The stock market can be volatile. It's a place of risk.

Don't worry that your emergency money isn't earning much interest or a big return. That's not its job.

I like to keep my savings in several different accounts.
Is that a good thing?

I'm a pot saver too. (No, not that kind of pot.) I like to keep
my money in various bank accounts because it helps me com-
partmentalize my finances and prevents crossover withdrawals. By this I mean that I don't touch the vacation pot for an
impulse purchase.

The rule is that you only touch the pot for its intended purpose — except in an emergency. One caveat to consider if you
like keeping money in numerous accounts, says Carolyn Mc-
Clanahan, a certified financial planner, is that "if a person dies
or becomes incapacitated, it becomes a bigger mess for the
family. Also, as people get older, they often lose track of old
accounts." So if you like having a lot of pots, be sure to keep
good records.

How safe is my money in the bank during a recession
or economic downturn?

Your bank deposit money is safe. The Federal Deposit Insurance Corporation, which is an independent federal agency
created by Congress, insures bank deposits, money market
accounts, and certificates of deposit (CDs). The FDIC insures
deposits only. It does not insure securities, mutual funds, or
similar types of investments that banks and thrift institutions
may offer.

Since the FDIC was created in 1933, no depositor has
lost a dollar of insured deposits. Accounts are insured up to
$250,000 per depositor, per insured bank, for each owner-
ship category.

To learn more about the safety of your deposits, go to fdic.
gov and search for "Are my deposits insured?"

The National Credit Union Share Insurance Fund
(NCUSIF), also backed by the federal government and man-
aged by the National Credit Union Administration, insures
credit union members' deposits in federal credit unions up to
$250,000. State-chartered credit unions may also be covered
by NCUSIF. Go to mycreditunion.gov to read more about the
safety of your deposits.

I know I need to save, but don't I deserve to treat myself every so often?

The answer to this question falls squarely on where your financial priorities lie.

In 2019, my eldest child experienced a spontaneous pneu-
mothorax, which is the sudden onset of a collapsed lung without any apparent cause. She was 24 and working in Houston as the resident social worker for a nonprofit that cares for
children who have been removed from their homes for various reasons. My daughter ended up needing surgery to repair
her right lung. She was hospitalized for nine days.

Without giving it a second thought, my husband and I
booked last-minute airline tickets to Houston. We reserved
a suite because our daughter ended up needing a few days of
extra care after she was released. We were able to do all of that
so quickly because we had saved the money to cover emergency expenses without going into debt.

Yes, you can treat yourself, but not before making sure you
have emergency funds saved for life's unexpected events. Our
trip to Houston put a significant dent in our "life happens"
fund, a hit my husband and I were happy to take so that we
could be there for our daughter.

It's okay to treat yourself, but not at the expense of building a savings account that needs to be there in a crisis. So, to answer the question, no, you don't get to splurge until you have a decent start on your emergency and "life happens" funds. You will thank me later.

Should I keep saving for retirement or my child's college education during a recession?

If you haven't had a disruption in your income, then yes, keep saving and investing.

When you're frightened, the natural instinct is to focus on your immediate needs and to stop thinking about the long term — in this case, to stop investing for something you need in the future. The problem is, once you pull back on those investments, it's hard to start back up again.

If you've lost your job, then it makes sense to stop saving and to concentrate on keeping a roof over your head and food on the table. Until there is a financial crisis, however, keep saving.

CREDIT

What should I do if I can't pay my credit card bill?

If you find yourself unable to pay your credit card bill, immediately contact the credit card issuer.

I know. You would rather not. You might think, *What's the point, because I don't have the money to pay the bill?* But you will only make matters worse by ignoring the issue. Make the call. Even if you can't pay in full, you can try to work out a payment plan or a settlement.

If you are trying to set up a payment plan, be honest with the credit card company and with yourself. Don't overpromise. If you can afford only $50 a month, tell your creditor. There's no point in agreeing to a payment plan that you know you can't sustain for more than a few months.

If you need help negotiating with your credit card companies, get help from a nonprofit credit counseling agency. You can find one by going to DebtAdvice.org.

I ran up my credit cards trying to stay afloat after
   losing my job and then couldn't pay them.
   What's the best way to improve my credit score?
The number one way to improve your credit score is to *pay your bills on time.* The FICO credit score model ranges from a low of 300 to a high of 850. Thirty-five percent of your score under the FICO credit scoring model is your payment history. Negative information such as failure to pay your credit card bills stays on your credit report for seven years, but the further away you get from the date of default, the less impact the old debt has on your credit score. As long as the most recent information on your credit report shows a history of on-time payments, your credit score will generally improve.

The second most effective way to improve your score is to pay down your debts. Thirty percent of your score is derived from how much you owe.

Together, these two actions — paying promptly and dumping your debt — will improve your credit score.

I fell behind on my credit cards, but a debt-relief
   company says it can help me reduce what I owe.
   Should I sign up with the company?

Absolutely not! Stay away from these companies. What you're
searching for is a microwave fix for a problem that takes some
time to resolve.

Debt-settlement or debt-relief service companies may
promise to work on your behalf, claiming that they are better
than you are at negotiating a deal to reduce your debts. The offer is enticing, especially if you're tired of getting creditor calls
or threatening default letters.

A good credit history leads to better rates for a car or home
loan. A bad credit history can leave you stuck with loans carrying high interest rates and other onerous terms. It's understandable that you want to try to repair your credit and as
quickly as possible. Yet this isn't the way.

I don't like so-called debt-relief companies for these reasons:

- **You are told to stop making any payments, even
  if you're current on the debt.** The idea behind this
  strategy is that you'll be saving money so that you can
  offer the creditor a lump-sum payoff for far less than you
  owe. But when you stop making payments as a part of
  a debt-settlement plan, you will likely trigger penalties,
  higher interest rates, and other fees, which will cause
  your balance to grow.
- **You are encouraged to cease communication with
  your creditors.** For scammers, this is just a way to delay
  your finding out that they are a sham.
- **You're given false hope and sometimes a guarantee**

that the company can negotiate a deal. In fact, many creditors won't even negotiate with debt-settlement firms. This means they are offering a service they can't possibly perform.

- **The service can cost thousands of dollars.** There isn't much these companies can do for you that you can't do for yourself. Besides, instead of paying their fees, you could use that money to pay down your debts.

And just so you know, companies that sell debt-relief services over the telephone are by law prohibited from collecting advance fees before they have completed the services they have promised. They also can't delete accurate negative information from your credit files, so don't believe any false claims that they can. The firms are legally prohibited from misrepresenting what they can do for debtors, such as promising that a certain percentage of your debt can be erased.

In 2019, the Consumer Financial Protection Bureau (CFPB) reached a $25 million settlement with a debt-relief company that the CFPB said violated the Federal Trade Commission's telemarketing sales rule by charging people in advance of debt-relief services. The CFPB said the company charged debtors without settling their debts and hid from customers that several major banks have a standing policy never to work with a debt-settlement company.

Listen to a podcast about an undercover investigation of debt-settlement companies by the U.S. Government Accountability Office (GAO). Go to gao.gov and search for "Fraudulent, Abusive, and Deceptive Practices Pose Risk to Consumers." In an accompanying report, the GAO provided examples of debt settlements that put borrowers in a worse situation.

- A North Carolina woman and her husband fell deeper into debt, filed for bankruptcy in an attempt to save their home from foreclosure, and took second jobs as janitors after paying $11,000 to two Florida companies for debt-settlement services that were never delivered.
- A couple from New York was profiled as a success story by an Arizona company even though the fees it charged plus the settled balance totaled more than 140 percent of what the couple originally owed.
- A 75-year-old New York woman ended up paying more than $5,100 to a company to settle only $3,900 of debt on one account.

During economic downturns, there is often a dramatic increase in the demand for debt-relief services, says the GAO. "Our investigation found that some debt settlement companies engage in fraudulent, deceptive, and abusive practices that pose a risk to consumers already in difficult financial situations."

Don't believe all the false hope many of these for-profit companies sell. Instead, get help from a nonprofit credit counseling agency. Go to DebtAdvice.org and search for an agency by your zip code. You can get help right over the phone.

How do I build my credit?

Get a secured credit card. This is one of the best ways to build credit if you have a thin credit file or you've had issues in the past with paying your bills on time.

Check with your bank or credit union to sign up for a secured credit card. You can also search for secured-card issuers at Bankrate.com. You will be required to deposit anywhere from $250 to $500 in a bank account. This money is the security for your credit line. So if you put up $250, your available credit line would be $250. The goal is to build a credit history and good credit score, so you don't need a high credit limit.

Make sure that the issuer is reporting your payment history to all three of the major credit bureaus — Equifax, Experian, and TransUnion.

My daughter established a credit history by signing up for a secured card through her credit union. Here's how she established a good credit history and score in a relatively short amount of time: She charged small-dollar-amount items on the secured card, which had a credit limit of $250. I suggested that she not charge more than about 10 percent of the available credit limit. In the case of a card with a $250 limit, that would be $25 in total in each billing cycle. She paid the balance off as soon as the pending charge was posted. (By the way, do not let anyone tell you that you should leave a small balance on the card to help build up your score. This is not true.) She was to pay every bill off on time. This was key.

Three months later, her credit score was 737. Six months after that, it was 743. At that point I recommended that she apply for a regular credit card, one where she did not have to keep money in a savings account as collateral in case she didn't pay the charges on the secured credit card. She was approved for a $2,500 credit limit. By that time her credit score was close to 750.

So, in about a year, she had built up a good credit history just by charging very little on the secured card.

I'm trying to help someone build up her credit history. Should I let her be an authorized user on my card?

The strategy of letting someone become an authorized user on your credit card is called piggybacking. People with no credit or bad credit are often encouraged to get their parent, grandparent, or friend to add them onto a credit card as an authorized user. The authorized user benefits from the positive credit history of the primary cardholder.

It's important to realize that the person who is piggybacking isn't liable for paying any of the charges he or she makes on the card. I've seen plenty of parents, siblings, and even girlfriends and boyfriends get stuck with a credit card bill after allowing someone to become an authorized user.

I received an email from a cardholder who had allowed her friend to become an authorized user on her credit card. The friend wanted to take advantage of a zero percent balance transfer offer. The friend transferred $3,500 in debt onto the card and promised to pay it off before the one-year promotional offer ended. The friend managed to pay only $700 of the debt before filing for bankruptcy protection. The cardholder ended up having to pay the remaining $2,800.

If you are going to use the piggybacking strategy, set a maximum limit that the authorized user can charge. Make sure it's a limit you can handle in case you get stuck with the debt.

I've lost my job and had to start using my credit card to make ends meet. How badly will this damage my credit history?

If you can manage to pay even the minimum amount due on your credit card and on time during your unemployment, the damage should be minimal. But as you approach or hit the credit limit, that can negatively affect your credit history.

You want to pay attention to your credit utilization rate or ratio, which is the amount of revolving credit you are using divided by the total amount of your available credit. You may have heard that you shouldn't use more than 30 percent of your available credit limit. For example, if your credit card limit is $1,000, you should keep your balance to $300 or less. This would apply for each individual credit card and the overall utilization for all your cards.

However, the 30 percent benchmark isn't a hard-and-fast rule. In fact, if you're striving for a perfect 850 credit score, you should aim for single-digit credit utilization. FICO, the company behind the most widely used credit score, says its research shows that those with a FICO score above 795 use on average 7 percent of their credit limit. The average revolving utilization for consumers with a perfect 850 credit score was about 4 percent.

In better times, of course, you want to keep the amount of debt you have to a minimum. However, even if you ran up your cards because you felt you had no choice, as you pay them down once you're in a better financial position, your score will increase.

My credit card company closed the account for a credit card I rarely use. Why would the company do that? I pay my bill off in full every month when I do use the card.

During economic downturns, credit issuers often cut credit limits or even cancel cards with little or no warning. This can be true even for consumers with excellent credit scores who are considered prime customers. During the Great Recession, a Federal Reserve loan survey found that 20 percent of lenders cut credit lines for customers with prime credit scores, and 60 percent reduced lines for subprime cardholders.

Credit card companies will close accounts or reduce credit lines as a way to lessen their risk during uncertain financial times. Even people with good credit who lose their job can end up defaulting on their debt. The companies therefore try to reduce the risk of having a lot of defaults by reducing or canceling cards that people haven't been using but might start to utilize if they get into a financial jam.

If your credit limit is reduced or your card is canceled, call and ask that your account be reinstated. However, if your request is denied, there should be minimal impact to your credit score. Also, you won't necessarily lose the positive credit history. Any account closed in good standing — meaning you had no late payments — will remain on your credit report for 10 years, according to Experian.

DEBT

Is there such a thing as good debt and bad debt?
No, there is only debt.

Let me ask you, during an economic crisis, or anytime for that matter, how does having debt make you feel? Good? Wonderful? Are you radiant when you schedule a payment?

I hate debt. I don't feel good about any of it, including my mortgage.

Following an appearance on NPR's *1A* program, Jared Bernstein, former chief economist to then vice president Joe Biden, sent me a direct message on Twitter: "Do you really hate all debt? Isn't there good debt and bad debt?" During a broadcast interview, I had told the NPR host, "If debt were a person, I'd slap it!" This led to a debate with Bernstein in our respective columns.

He said, "I think there's great debt, good debt, and bad debt. Great debt boosts your earning power such that you can pay it back and have money left over afterward to safely take on some good debt, by which I mean debt that raises your living standards, if not your earning power. A student loan can be (that's *can be*, not *is*) great debt. A home loan can be good debt."

I said, "Without mortgages, most Americans couldn't afford to purchase a home, which for many households ends up being their biggest asset. I recognize that business loans have helped people follow their passions and create small businesses. But what we need in America is not more cheerleading of debt but more caution. When I speak about debt with a deep hatred, I'm purposely targeting the folks prone to irrational financial optimism. I'm trying to help them put on the brakes. If you hate debt, as I do, you'll approach it with trepidation. You'll be careful not to take on too much, because you loathe it. And if you disdain debt, you'll do what you can to get rid of it as soon as you can."

In my opinion, there is no good debt.

Should I pay off my credit cards before I save?
You need to do both, pay off debt *and* save. If you focus only on paying off debt and you don't have any savings, then when an emergency comes up, you'll end up borrowing money from a friend or relative or running up your credit cards again. You need to have a cash cushion that comes from saving.

If your job is secure and you have a lot of debt, just save enough so that you have a decent amount in your emergency fund and "life happens" fund. For example, while you're continuing to pay down your debts, save $1,000 into your "life happens" fund. If you have to withdraw money from the account, build it back up to $1,000, then stop and concentrate on paying off your debts.

Likewise, set an initial goal of saving one month's worth of household expenses in your emergency fund. Once you hit that benchmark, stop and concentrate on getting out of debt.

What's the best way to pay off my debts?

The math says you should pay off the debt that has the highest interest rate, because you will shell out less money. But based on my experience, mind over money works better. Research backs this up.

Borrowers are more motivated to get out of debt when they concentrate first on the debt with the smallest balance, according to a 2016 study published in the *Journal of Consumer Research*. I find that when people can pay off a debt quickly, they get excited and speed up their payoff timetable. This often results in less interest paid overall.

There are various names for this debt payoff model, but I call mine the "debt dash." Taking this approach, you list all your debt obligations, starting with the one with the lowest balance, so smallest to largest. If two debts are about the same amount, the one with the higher interest rate gets priority treatment. Then look for any extra money you can find in your budget and apply it to the smallest debt at the top of the list while you continue making the minimum payments on all the other debts.

Once you've knocked off the debt at the top of the list, pat yourself on the back. You did it! Then start paying down the second debt on your list. You do this by adding all the money you had already been paying on the first debt. Before you know it, the second debt will be gone too! Keep following the debt dash until all your debts are paid off.

By the way, make sure that your extra payments are applied to the principal and not counted as an additional monthly payment.

Isn't it okay to borrow money for college? Doesn't that pay for itself eventually?

My husband and I started planning for the cost of college when our kids were tiny people. I could say that the only motivation was to be sure they could go to college debt-free. But the truth is I wanted them to become independent and stay independent so I can kiss my husband in my own home without hearing *ewww* sounds from my kids.

Student loan debt has become a serious national issue. Nationwide, outstanding student loans crossed the trillion-dollar mark at the end of 2011. That figure has been climbing ever since, making some people wonder if college is worth it at all.

For many families, college comes at the expense of decades of debt. Most college expense is funded through student loans, but 24 percent of people have borrowed with credit cards and 7 percent with a home equity line of credit, according to the Federal Reserve.

Economists and researchers have long argued that a college degree — even with debt — is worth it, pointing to a "college income premium." Workers with a bachelor's degree on

average earn well over $1 million more than high school grad-
uates during their working lives, according to a 2014 report
by the Federal Reserve. However, that income premium is being eroded by wage stagnation.

You need to plan very carefully for paying for your kids' college tuition bills so that neither you nor they are saddled with
debts that never seem to go away.

I know I have student loans, but I need a vacation. If I save for the vacation, can I go?

I once wrote a column with the headline "If You're in Debt,
You Don't Deserve a Vacation." By the readers' responses, you
would have thought I had claimed that the earth was flat.

You could go away on vacation, but the financially prudent
thing is to plow through your debt first. Again, it's about setting financial priorities.

Often people talk themselves into spending by saying
things like "I deserve a vacation . . . because I work hard." I'm
not saying you don't deserve to relax, but not at the expense
of making headway with your debts or saving for a rainy
day. The money you're "saving" for a vacation should really
be your debt relief fund. And the more savings and the less
debt you have, the better prepared you will be to weather the
next financial crisis, because there certainly will be another.
Don't take a break from building up your emergency fund
and "life happens" fund or from paying off debt to treat yourself.

Can I be honest? I want you to suffer. Because it's in your
struggle and self-denial that you learn self-control. Debt is
debilitating. If you suffer enough during the payoff process,
you are less likely to go back into debt — ever.

Do I have to pay off old debts that still show up on my credit report?

Watch out for zombie debt collectors. They won't eat your brain, but they will try to revive debt that is by law too old for any court action.

Dishonest debt collection companies often try to scare you into paying a debt that is "time-barred." Creditors have a limited number of years in which they can take you to court to collect on an unsecured debt, such as past-due credit card charges. After that time runs out, certain unpaid, open-ended consumer debts are considered time-barred. You still owe the money, but after a period of several years, your old debt becomes uncollectible through the courts.

The statute of limitations for time-barred debt varies from state to state — anywhere from two to ten years. If you want to check on the law for your state, the legal website nolo.com has a good guide. Search for "Civil Statutes of Limitations."

If the debt is too old to collect, the best thing is simply to do nothing. Don't promise to make payments, which could restart the collection process and expose you to legal action.

On the other hand, if you have the money, you can offer to make a lump-sum payment to that creditor, often for far less than the defaulted amount. Once it's paid, keep the letter or email about the negotiated payoff and your canceled check or receipt forever in case there's ever a question about that debt in the future. Old debt is often resold, and your payoff information may get lost in the process.

Should I file for bankruptcy to get rid of my debts?

The Bankruptcy Abuse Prevention and Consumer Protection Act of 2005 has made it tougher for people to discharge their debts under Chapter 7. In a Chapter 7 bankruptcy, you can erase many of your unsecured debts, such as payday loans and credit card, medical, and old utility bills. Some debts can't be erased, such as child support, certain taxes, and government fines and penalties. Student loans are extremely difficult to get rid of in bankruptcy.

Before filing for a Chapter 7 bankruptcy, debtors are required to get credit counseling, which will include discussing other options to filing for bankruptcy. A list of approved nonprofit credit counseling agencies can be found on the U.S. Trustee Program website at justice.gov/ust. Click on the link for "Credit Counseling & Debtor Education." You also need to complete a debtor education course, which is intended to equip you with money management tips and tools, after you file for bankruptcy.

You must pass a means test in order to file under Chapter 7. Don't be overly concerned about the means test. Most debtors qualify, but it does weed out people who could afford to repay their creditors. When you apply for a Chapter 7, the court will compare your current monthly income with the median income for a family of your size in your state. What's important is your "disposable income," or what you have left from your paycheck after certain expenses are allowed by the court.

If you earn too much to file under Chapter 7, you can file under Chapter 13, which requires debtors to pay back some of their debt over a five-year period. One major advantage of Chapter 13 is that you can save your home from foreclosure. You're allowed to catch up with past-due payments by entering into a repayment plan. In a Chapter 7 you might be able to delay a foreclosure, but you must be current on your mort-

gage payments to keep the home. Bankruptcy is a complicated process, so please seek legal advice.

Bankruptcy also isn't cheap. There are filing fees, of course,
and the expense of hiring an attorney. The national average
for a Chapter 7 filing is $1,250, according to the National
Bankruptcy Forum. The cost can vary depending on where
you live and the complexity of your case. Attorney fees for a
Chapter 13 filing on average are about $3,000. Contact your
local legal aid society to check whether you qualify for free
help, the Forum recommends.

If your debts are overwhelming, you should investigate
whether bankruptcy is right for you. Since filers must get pre-
bankruptcy credit counseling, you can access that by going
to nfcc.org, the site for the National Foundation for Credit
Counseling, or calling 1-800-388-2227.

*I had to file for bankruptcy in the past because of bad
decisions I made. This time my financial situation
isn't my fault. Can I file again if I lose my job and
can't pay my bills?*

Thankfully, nowadays being broke doesn't end in a debtor's
prison sentence. But in 2005, Congress did make it tougher
to completely erase your debts if you have the ability to repay
your creditors.

It's understandable that your debts can pile up following a
financial crisis or after a job loss if there's a recession or economic downturn. But be aware that there are limits on how
soon you can file again. After your first Chapter 7 bankruptcy,
you must wait eight years before you can file a second time.
You have to wait two years before you can file a Chapter 13

again. If you file a Chapter 13, you need to wait six years before you can file under Chapter 7. The wait is four years if you're seeking to file a Chapter 13 after having filed a Chapter 7.

For more basics about bankruptcy, go to the website for the National Consumer Law Center and search for "Answers to Common Bankruptcy Questions."

By the way, filing for bankruptcy isn't a credit death sentence. You can still qualify for credit after a bankruptcy. In fact, not long after your bankruptcy is discharged you may start getting offers for credit.

Bankruptcy should be used as a last resort, but if your debts become overwhelming, it's an option that you should explore. Be sure to check out the section in this book that focuses on your credit.

DEBT COLLECTION – YOUR RIGHTS

A debt collector is threatening to sue me. What are my rights?

The Fair Debt Collection Practices Act provides certain rights for debtors. For example, debt collectors can't lie to you. They can't say they'll take you to court and garnish your wages unless they are allowed by law to take such action and intend to do so.

If you are having a problem with a debt collection company, file a complaint with the Consumer Financial Protection Bureau. Go to consumerfinance.gov and click on the link for "Submit a Complaint."

You will find a lot of information about your rights as a debtor at the Federal Trade Commission's website, ftc.gov. Search for "Debt Collection FAQs."

I know I owe on a past debt, but the amount the
company says I owe is much more than I recall.
Can I make the debt collection company prove how
much I owe?

Yes, it is your right to ask the company to provide proof of the
debt. Quite frankly, many can't.

A debt collector must tell you how much you owe and the
name of the creditor and what you can do if you don't think
the debt is yours. Once you send a letter disputing the debt
or asking for verification, the company must stop contacting you. However, it can start the collection process again if it
then sends written verification. But many times the debt company may have only scant information, such as your name,
last known address, Social Security number, and the proposed
debt amount. Without billing statements or an original contract or credit card application with your signature, it's unlikely the debt collection company can prove the debt is yours.

Before agreeing to settle a debt, verify that the debt is truly
yours and what you owe. Ask for the date of the last payment
so that you can double-check whether the statute of limitations has expired.

Go to Bankrate.com and search for "Statute of limitations
on debts by state."

A debt collection company is calling my job. Is that
legal? How do I stop the collection calls?

Under the Fair Debt Collection Practices Act, debt collectors
can't contact you at all hours of the day and night. They can't
call before 8 a.m. or after 9 p.m. You can request for the company to stop calling your place of employment if you aren't
allowed to get calls on your job. You can also send a letter —

I recommend certified mail or Return Receipt to prove you sent it — to ask that the debt collection firm stop contacting you. (Of course, this does not cancel the debt.)

The federal Consumer Financial Protection Bureau has sample letters you can send to a debt collector, including one requesting that the firm stop the calls. Go to consumerfinance.gov and search for "What should I do when a debt collector contacts me?" There are several debt-collection letter templates you can download, including:

- I want the debt collector to stop contacting me.
- I need more information about this debt.
- I do not owe this debt.

Where can I get help to fight a creditor or landlord in court?

Most importantly, *do not* ignore any court action. You need to show up in court to avoid a default judgment. Do your best to find legal help.

In the case of an eviction proceeding, the vast majority of landlords — 90 percent — show up in housing court with an attorney, while tenants often face eviction without legal counsel, according to the Center for American Progress.

Go to LawHelp.org to find free legal aid programs in your community.

What should I do if I don't owe the debt?

Send the debt collector a letter saying that you don't owe any money and ask for verification. The debt collection company has to send you proof, such as a copy of a bill.

The Federal Trade Commission has a lot of information that explains your rights as a debtor. Go to ftc.gov and search for "Debt Collection FAQs."

My only income is from Social Security. Can a debt collector take part of my Social Security check?

A creditor or debt collector can take you to court to get a judgment for nonpayment. The court may order your bank to take money from your bank account to pay the debt. But certain federal benefits, such as Social Security, Supplemental Security Income (SSI), and veterans' benefits, are off-limits and are typically exempt from garnishment.

During the Great Recession, the Social Security Administration's inspector general found that some institutions were violating federal law by garnishing accounts that received electronic deposits of Old Age, Survivors, and Disability Insurance and/or Supplemental Security Income payments. "Millions of beneficiaries rely on Social Security benefits as their only source of income for basic needs such as housing and food," the inspector general's report said. "When a creditor's garnishment order is enforced and these Federal funds withheld, the lives of a vulnerable segment of the population are placed at risk."

The report also found that in some cases banks were charging overdraft and other fees that occurred as the result of a garnishment.

Social Security benefits can, though, be garnished to pay for defaulted student loans — even those taken out for the benefit of your adult children or grandchildren.

Additionally, a financial institution can take benefits to hand over to creditors to collect child support and/or alimony or unpaid federal taxes as the result of an IRS levy. Up to 15 percent of monthly payments can be taken until the debt is paid.

If your benefits have been wrongly taken from your bank account or a creditor tries to garnish your Social Security check, alert the financial institution that what it is doing is illegal.

The Past

You can't go back in time and change what you've already done, but if you start to ask the right questions going forward, you can change your habit of making bad financial decisions.

I've worked with hundreds of people who have opened up their books and financial lives for me to explore. In just about every case, I have been able to trace issues with how they handle their money to their personal backstory or the things they dealt with growing up.

A married father of two young children struggles with being a spendthrift because he remembers the haunting experience of poverty. He knew hunger. He recalls coming home from school and the lights being cut off. His wife, wanting to help him feel loved, enables his overspending so that he doesn't relive his childhood deprivation. Or someone else I worked with was given everything she ever wanted, not realizing that her parents were going broke in order to keep up the lie that they had more than enough.

A financial crisis can throw you off your game through no fault of your own. However, if you've dealt with the demons that dictated your earlier spending habits, you might have been able to handle a financial crisis.

The past holds the answer to a lot of questions about why

you do what you do with your money. Your history doesn't have to define your financial future. But in order to change, you have to acknowledge some experiences from your past that you may have forgotten about or even buried. Many of the answers that follow are intended to help you understand and address your backstory issues in the hope that you'll be better prepared for the next financial crisis.

I grew up poor, so it's hard to deny myself or my children. How do I overcome my past?

Before I answer this question, I'd like to tell you a little about my own childhood.

At four, I went to live with my grandmother, whom we affectionately called Big Mama. My grandmother ended up caring for my four siblings as well. I had two sisters, eight and three at the time, and one-year-old twin brothers. In a single day, the five of us became my grandmother's responsibility. Before we came to live with Big Mama, she said she had a dream that we were in trouble. The next morning, she sent my grandfather to do a welfare check on us. We were home alone, with literally nothing to eat in the refrigerator. The five of us were huddled in one room, scared and crying. My grandfather, Papa, took us home with him, and we never lived with our parents again.

I've seen my father about half a dozen times in my life. My mother was in and out of our lives. She was unreliable and frankly toxic at times. Although we eventually reconciled, I've spent much of my life seeking to fill the void left by her unreliable presence.

Big Mama took great care of us, but as you can imagine, suddenly becoming the caregiver for five grandchildren was a struggle for her. My grandmother was an amazing money manager, but things were tight, especially since my grandfather had a drinking problem and his paycheck often ended up in the cash registers of local bars in Baltimore.

This is just a small part of my financial backstory. And it explains a lot about why I'm so frugal. Although I was just four when I went to live with my grandparents, I remember being hungry. I recall when I was a little older waiting for my mother to show up on Christmas Day, only to be disappointed when she canceled. Or, worse, I recall those times when she didn't cancel at all. She left me and my siblings looking out the window for hours on Christmas and on other occasions — birthdays — in eager anticipation of her visit and the gifts she had promised.

My mother's no-shows left some deep psychological scars, which I've had to work through in therapy. Maybe you had a similar background, and as a result you're a spendthrift, shopping all the time to soothe the pain. Or, like me, you have chosen the opposite, becoming a super-saver, always worried about your financial security.

Where am I going with all this? Your past is part of who you are, but it doesn't have to dictate your future, especially when it comes to your money. Often people try to overcompensate for what they didn't get as a child. They overspend on themselves or their children or both.

If you grew up in poverty, with hand-me-down clothes or missed meals — or an unreliable parent — it's understandable that you want your children never to feel deprived, even if it means you go broke trying to make sure they want for nothing. But you can't buy back a better childhood for yourself no matter how much you give to your children.

This is what I tell parents struggling to give their children a better life experience: It's about your presence, not the presents. Your children need you to be present in their lives. They need you to be loving, consistent, and financially responsible. They need you to be the adult and plan for when times won't be so good financially.

As a child I may have whined about not getting a Barbie doll, but what I really needed was just the love of a mother and father who I could count on to be there for me. Children may nag about getting the latest electronic device or toy, but years later, as mature adults, when the memory of what they begged for has faded, they'll recall whether they felt safe, heard, and valued. You can't purchase the things that are priceless.

I'll be honest. As a child, I thought Big Mama was pretty cruel when we begged for stuff our friends had and she ignored our pleas. She would even fuss about our requests. But she never felt bad about what she couldn't buy for us, because she knew she provided the essentials.

It wasn't until I had my own children that I understood the reason behind what I thought was her unreasonable frugality. Even though my husband and I could afford to give our three children so much more, we chose to give them material things in moderation compared to the stuff they complained that their friends were receiving in abundance. We wanted our children to learn about living *below* our means, so that when they became adults, they would understand the concept of contentment. We wanted to create the mindset that they could start out living *within* their own means and not try to recreate a lifestyle they couldn't afford.

The trap of overindulging your children can happen at any income level. Do too much and you risk creating entitled adults. According to a survey by Credit Karma, an online site that provides free credit scores and consumer financial information, most parents (53 percent) used debt — credit cards or bank loans – to pay for nonessential items (designer clothes, cell phones, cosmetic care) or experiences (concerts, musicals, or theater) for their kids. About three out of five parents (61 percent) felt peer pressure to spend money they didn't have to buy nonessentials for their children.

My husband and I preached to our kids about delayed gratification and modeled it for them. And now, as young adults, they all are savers and savvy shoppers.

If you're living from paycheck to paycheck, do your best to make do with what you have. Don't feel embarrassed about what you can't give to your children. Explain to them in an age-appropriate way what you *can* afford. Don't burden your children, but also don't hide the truth of your struggle.

If a financial crisis sets you back, as it has done for so many people as a result of the COVID-19 crisis, don't try to make up for what you have lost by overspending if and when you get back to solid financial ground. You do more harm than good when you spoil your children. Remember that the word *spoil* means to make rotten.

I'm just bad at money management. What can I do to be better?

I'm not a trained therapist, but I've helped enough people with their finances to know that good money management starts with an analysis of why you do what you do. It's about what's going on in your mind, not necessarily how much money you have.

For this question, forget about the budget and all the numbers. First examine why you're bad with budgeting. Write down your financial backstory. I mean it. Stop right here. Put the book down just for a bit, and start jotting down memories of your childhood. What financial story does it tell? Did you have a difficult childhood? What money lessons did you learn or not learn as a child? Did your parents argue about money? Did you resent not being able to get the gifts and things your friends had? How did your parents or parent handle money?

You've got to become self-aware before you can become a better steward of your money. If you can't do this yourself, get some help. Get some therapy.

I understand that even mentioning therapy may set you on edge. But I'm a big believer in working with a mental health professional to help unlock the things that are blocking you from managing your money well.

Under Obamacare, mental and behavioral health services are a required essential benefit for plans in the health-care marketplace. If you don't have access to a health plan that offers therapy, you can find help at Federally Qualified Health Centers, which are funded by the federal government's Health Resources and Services Administration, an agency of the Department of Health and Human Services. To find a health center, go to bphc.hrsa.gov. You may also find some resources at MentalHealth.gov. If your income is low enough, you may qualify for Medicaid.

There is also the National Alliance on Mental Illness (nami. org), which offers a help line that provides information, resource referrals, and support to individuals and families. Call 1-800-950-6264 or send an email to info.nami.org.

If your issues aren't that deep and it's just a matter of math phobia, then get help from a budget counselor, who can help you develop better money management habits. You can find a nonprofit credit counseling agency at nfcc.org, which is run by the National Foundation for Credit Counseling.

The one thing you shouldn't do is keep telling yourself that you're bad at money management and then do nothing about it. You need to change your internal dialogue and the way in which you handle your dollars.

I'm good at making bad financial decisions. What tips do you have to help me make better decisions when it comes to my money?

In order to make better decisions you need a system. Far too often financial decisions are made too quickly or are based on emotions. Sound decision-making requires that you leave your feelings out of it.

For example, you might have purchased a time-share property because you were feeling good on your vacation and saw it as a way to continue the fun in the future. Now that time-share is a financial albatross in your life. If you had had a step-by-step guide, you probably would have realized that buying the time-share was an impulsive decision that you'd later regret, especially if a financial crisis hits and you can't afford the loan payment and/or yearly maintenance fee.

The best defense against a relentless sales pitch is a system that slows down the decision.

Can you promise me something? Before you make a decision, follow the five steps below to a better outcome. And by *follow*, I don't mean look them over, shake your head, say, "Yeah, this sounds great," and then keep doing what you've been doing — that is, making decisions on the fly. If you want to stop making bad decisions, you've got to develop some discipline. I don't make any major decision without going through the following steps:

1. **Determine if the decision is a need or a want.** You need to get your car fixed if it breaks down. You may not need a new car. The reason you immediately start thinking it is time to buy a new or new-to-you (used) car is that you're tired of fixing your jalopy. Yet that could be the most cost-effective decision.

2. **Make a decision with your head, not your heart.** You are riding in the cab of the tow truck and you're very frustrated to have been stranded. However, this is not the time to vow, *I've had it, I'm buying a new car.*

   I dare say making the decision about whom to marry should be done with more logic than love, because divorce is a costly endeavor. If you had gone through a sound decision-making process, you might have saved yourself a lot of money and heartache.

   Can I share with you one of the reasons I married my husband? He was a good handyman. I purchased my first home — a two-bedroom, one-bath condo — a year after graduating from college. Not long after I moved in my toilet broke. Not wanting to pay for a plumber, I asked my then boyfriend if he knew anything about repairing a toilet. He had me at "Sure, I can fix your toilet." I married that man for his handyman skills — and for love too, of course.

3. **Consider all the alternatives.** Have you carefully considered other options? Let's stick with the decision to fix or buy a car. Instead of replacing the car, could you repair it? Is sharing a car, carpooling, or public transportation a viable option?

4. **Consider all the costs.** The numbers will almost always tell you if a financial move is right. A $1,200 car repair

bill is more than enough to get your heart racing. But buying a $40,000 car costs a lot more. How many monthly payments on that car will it take to exceed the $1,200 repair bill? Two? Three? Consider how long your auto loan may be. An increasing percentage of car buyers are opting to stretch their monthly car payments far longer than the traditional four-year auto loan. Even if you opt to purchase a low-priced used car, you still may face costly repairs. There is something to be said about the devil you know.

I have a bonus piece of advice. Once you finish paying off your auto loan, don't incorporate that money back into your budget. Take that monthly payment and stash it into a savings account. You can then use that money for repairs or eventually to pay cash for your next car.

If you're keeping an older car, be sure to have a mechanic check it out regularly. You'll save more money by catching mechanical problems early. Also, don't ignore warning lights on your dashboard.

5. **Get unbiased advice.** Staying with the car decision, it makes no sense to me that the only person you may talk to about the purchase is the salesperson selling you the car. You ought to have a file folder full of information (this dates me a bit — making notes on your mobile device is okay too) even before you set foot onto a dealership lot. Never base your decision only on the word of someone — the car salesman, for example — who has a financial stake in your making an uninformed decision.

I never learned how to manage money from my parents. Any tips on how to overcome a family history of bad money managers?

I have always been a good money manager, thanks to my grandmother, but she also left me with a lot of emotional baggage. She scared me into being a saver. My grandmother worried about having enough money all the time, even when she was financially secure. As a result, I'm still a money worrier. I have trouble spending even when I've saved for something. This may be the opposite of your issue, but the outcome is similar — a block to a healthy relationship with one's money.

At some point I decided I couldn't continue to blame my parents or grandmother for my issues, so I sought counseling, which has helped me conquer my fear of not having enough.

Because there will always be another financial crisis, you should take a class, see a mental health professional, or stick to a system that helps you make better financial decisions. Just do something to help the adult you to overcome your inner child and manage your money better.

I know I shouldn't spend so much on my children because money is tight, but can't I still splurge every now and then? If I'm too frugal, won't they grow up to be spenders?

I worried a lot that my children would be spendthrifts as adults because of my thriftiness. From the time my kids began asking for stuff, I started their money lessons. My husband and I developed rules to teach them to be money-wise. For example, they could not put anything in a shopping cart at the grocery store without knowing the price and having compared the cost to that of similar items.

Once there was a craft fair at my kids' school. My eldest daughter was excited about buying a dreamcatcher. Before she left for school, I pulled her aside and lectured her on the topic of price negotiations. "Whatever the person offers, you should make a counteroffer," I told my elementary-school child. Frustrated with my bargain shopping strategies, my child said, "Mommy, why are you always talking about money?" In response, I said, "It's my full-time job to make sure you are a good steward of your money." Without missing a beat, she retorted, "Well, can you make it your part-time job?"

No, you can't let up. You should be relentless about teaching your children how to live within a budget. But being thrifty doesn't mean they can't have fun. Be creative.

I get it. It's hard to say no when they are looking up at you, asking to have what their friends have. You don't want them to stand out because of what you can't afford to get them. Still, your full-time job is to be pennywise, because it's in the best interests of your children in the long term.

I'm not worried about a financial crisis. I earn a good salary, so why shouldn't I live the good life?

I defer to Benjamin Franklin on this issue. The government didn't put his face on the $100 bill for nothing.

Some of Franklin's most famous maxims about money can be found in his 1758 essay, "The Way to Wealth." The Project Gutenberg e-book can be found for free by searching online. The essay begins with the fictitious Father Abraham, who has been asked to speak to a crowd waiting for an auction to start. Father Abraham, quoting Poor Richard, lectures about several issues, including conspicuous consumption. Although the language is dated, Franklin's warnings are timeless.

- "If you would be wealthy, think of saving, as well as of getting."
- "Away, then, with your expensive follies, and you will not have then so much reason to complain of hard times."
- "When you have bought one fine thing you must buy ten more, that your appearance may be all of a piece."

Look, you don't want to live like a miser, but denying yourself in the present for the benefit of your own future financial safety is paramount. The good times are great until the bad times come. Leading up to the Great Recession, a lot of people argued with my stance on striving to save three to six months' worth of living expenses in an emergency fund. It's hard for me to get people to save when they actually have the money to put away. But even those who had healthy savings found that they still didn't have enough when the novel coronavirus caused thousands of businesses to shut down.

You could argue, of course, that if your savings will get depleted anyway, why deny yourself? The practice of saving in anticipation of a major storm is like having the sandbags used to prevent or reduce floodwater damage. Sandbags can act as a barrier to protect you and your property from damage during a flood. Water may still get into your home, but not as much if the sandbags are properly filled and smartly placed. The same principle applies to a savings account. You'll be glad to have that account in place and full of saved money when the financial storm comes.

The Present

The first sentence of a 2020 survey conducted by NPR, the Robert Wood Johnson Foundation, and Harvard's T.H. Chan School of Public Health put it succinctly: "The coronavirus outbreak has had unprecedented, widespread impacts on households across America." The COVID-19 recession upended the lives of American workers. Millions lost their jobs or experienced reduced work hours. In just three months during the pandemic, unemployment rose higher than it did over a two-year period during the Great Recession, according to the Pew Research Center.

Over the course of my career, I have been a staunch advocate for saving for an emergency. Then the coronavirus pandemic hit. Even those who heeded the advice to prepare for the worst didn't realize how bad it could get. You can save for a rainy day, but if you receive hurricane-force rain in the form of a job loss leading to sustained unemployment, you may still not have enough. Or perhaps you are close to retirement or are retired. You're worried about getting through a recession that has disrupted your carefully crafted retirement budget.

What follows are some of the questions I've most frequently received during severe economic downturns.

ON THE JOB

I'm close to retirement, and the uncertain economy has me worried about whether I can still retire. What would you suggest I do?

One of the things I've found in helping people with their finances is that they set benchmarks without knowing how they will reach them and whether the targets are realistic. This is often the case when it comes to a planned retirement date.

How do you know you are "close" to retirement? Did you pick the date based on the year you want to leave the workforce? Or did you run the numbers to see if and when you would be financially ready for retirement?

You may have noticed that "run the numbers" is a common edict from me. This is for a good reason: because most people don't run the numbers.

Let's take retirement for an example. I met a woman who was adamant that she was going to leave her federal government job when she was 56, the earliest age allowed for her to start collecting her federal pension. We had this exchange:

> *Me:* How did you pick that age?
> *Her:* Under FERS [the Federal Employees Retirement System], I can retire at 56. Besides, I'm tired of working and thought it was a good time to retire.
> *Me:* So how much will you be getting from your pension every month?
> *Her:* I'm not sure. I'll have to check.
> *Me:* How much do you have in your Thrift Savings Plan [TSP]?
> *Her:* I'm not sure, but I think about $150,000.

Me: What's your retirement budget like? Will your early
    pension be enough to cover all your expenses?

Her: Well, I haven't figured out the budget yet.

Me: What's your investment strategy for your retirement
    plan once you retire? How are your TSP funds
    invested? Do you need to change anything? Do you
    have enough cash reserves to *handle* a significant dip
    in the stock market?

Her: I have no idea what you're talking about.

Finally,

Me: So you don't really know if you can retire at 56, do
    you?

Her: Nope.

I relate this exchange to you because the timing of your retirement should be predicated on running the numbers to determine whether you're ready, regardless of whether the economy is in a crisis.

Now, if you've reviewed your finances and they looked good
before there was an economic downturn, figure out what
may have changed that could delay your retirement. For instance, perhaps you haven't saved enough outside your tax-
advantaged retirement account so that you don't have to tap
the funds at a time when the value of your investments has
dropped. If you don't have a good emergency fund, you might
need to work an extra year or two if you are able.

Experts recommend that you should have one to two years'
worth of emergency funds available in retirement so you don't
have to withdraw money from your investment account. If

you don't have to tap into those funds, you can stay the course and wait out a recession or an economic crisis until the stock market stabilizes.

What bothered me about the woman I spoke to was that she didn't have a good grasp of her retirement income and expenses. I thought that with just $150,000 in the Thrift Savings Plan, which is the federal government's version of a 401(k), she should work longer to save more. This would have been my advice even if there weren't a recession or an economic downturn.

Also, by retiring early she was going to get a little less every month in her pension check. She still had a mortgage, and retiring wouldn't really lower her expenses as much as she thought. Let's say she had to regularly tap the $150,000 in the TSP to supplement her federal pension. The earliest she can start collecting Social Security is at age 62. Considering a conservative average annual 5 percent rate of return before taxes and a federal marginal tax bracket of 25 percent, if she withdrew $2,000 a month, the harsh reality is that she'd run out of funds in about seven years.

If you are thinking about retirement and want to run your own numbers, Mutual of Omaha has a very simple calculator on how long your money will last. Visit mutualofomaha .com/advice/calculator/how-long-will-my-money-last.   You can find similar calculators by searching online for "How long will my retirement savings last?" or "Retirement Longevity Calculator." Of course, if you're married or living with a partner, any decision to retire should include factoring in the impact of your retirement on the overall household income.

Keep in mind, the day you retire doesn't mean you have to withdraw all your retirement money. In fact, that would be foolish. It's possible you could live 20 to 30, maybe even 40 years in retirement, which would give your portfolio time to recover from a bear stock market (which is a decline of at least 20 percent from its previous peak; a bull market is defined as a 20 percent increase in the stock market from the previous low).

An economic crisis is a scary time. And yet you can't let fear lead your decisions. You also don't want to let it derail solid plans.

There are signs that there may be layoffs at my job. If I am laid off, should I cash out my retirement account?

It's very tempting to take the money. But in the moment — even during dire times — you should consider the long-term impact of cashing out your retirement account.

One major reason to let the money be is that you may not net as much as you think if you take some or all of it now. If you're younger than 59½, you must pay a 10 percent early withdrawal penalty. On top of that, you must pay the income taxes. Wells Fargo has an online calculator to help you determine how much in taxes you could owe if you take an early distribution from your retirement plan; visit wellsfargo .com/investing/retirement/tools/401k-early-withdrawal -calculator.

Let's say you have $45,000 in your retirement account. You're 45 and plan to retire at 65. Your federal income tax rate is 24 percent and the state tax rate (if you're subject to one) is 6 percent. The calculator will ask you to indicate the expected rate of return on your retirement account. I selected a conservative return of 5 percent. If you decided to cash out the entire $45,000, here's what to expect:

- $4,500 early withdrawal penalty
- $9,000 required federal withholding (generally the IRS requires an up-front automatic 20 percent withholding for federal taxes)
- $3,600 in additional federal taxes you may owe
- $2,700 in state taxes

In this case you'd end up forking over 44 percent of the money, or $19,800, to the government. You'd receive only $25,200, or 56 percent, of the original $45,000. But if you left the money to grow over 20 years, until you reach 65, the potential future value of your $45,000 could be $119,398, according to the Wells Fargo calculator. You could end up with even more, depending on how you invest.

Wells Fargo notes that the 10-year average rate of return for the S&P 500 index was 13.84 percent annually as of July 2020. During the same period the Dow Jones Industrial Average returned an average of 12.48 percent annually. As always, past performance is not a guarantee of future results.

There is a little-known IRS rule that allows workers to avoid the 10 percent penalty. If you leave or lose your job in the year you turn 55 or later (it's 50 for certain public safety employees, such as police officers), you aren't subject to the 10 percent penalty. The rule does not apply to an IRA or funds in a retirement account with a past employer.

There are some additional exceptions to the IRS early withdrawal penalty. You can avoid the penalty if you're disabled, incur eligible medical expenses, or have childbirth or adoption expenses. You may also duck the penalty by taking what the IRS calls substantially equal periodic payments (SEPP). Go to irs.gov and search for "Exceptions to Tax on Early Distributions" for a chart on the various ways to avoid the penalty.

If you've lost your job and are looking at your retirement funds to help pay the bills, consider the following:

- **Wait to see if you really need the money.** You may find that you can get by without taking a withdrawal. At least make it a last resort.
- **Take only what you need.** If you feel this really is your last resort, don't take all the money. If you've exhausted all other options — unemployment benefits, savings, financial gifts from family and friends — withdraw just enough to make ends meet.
- **Leave the money alone.** Hard times call for desperate measures. Still, try to exhaust other options before tapping your retirement account during a financial crisis.

I'm being laid off. Should I get a master's degree to better my chances of finding another job?

I'm not a fan of debt, as you may have discerned by now. I understand the desire to improve your skills to make yourself more marketable. However, tread carefully in racking up debt for a college education or to earn another degree.

I've met a lot of people during my years as a personal finance columnist who thought that getting a master's degree would help them get a better-paying job. But what they ended up with was a lot of graduate school loans — often in the six figures — that didn't lead to an increase in their earnings. And if they did end up earning more, a lot of the additional income went to paying off their student loans.

The payoff of earning a master's degree can vary greatly. "In some occupations, workers with a master's degree earned about the same as, or even less than, those with a bachelor's degree," the Bureau of Labor Statistics warns. In other fields — science, technology, math, engineering, education, and some medical fields (including medical doctors), an advanced degree does pay off.

Sixty percent of students who completed a master's degree in 2015–2016 had student loan debt from either undergraduate or graduate school, according to the National Center for Education Statistics. Among those with student loan debt, the average balance was $66,000.

The Gallup Alumni Survey, formerly referred to as the Gallup-Purdue Index, has been evaluating the long-term success of graduates. In a 2018 survey of more than 4,000 adults who received a postgraduate degree between 2000 and 2015, Gallup found that only 42 percent of graduates with a master of business administration (MBA) degree felt it was worth the cost. An astonishingly low percentage of graduates with a law degree (23 percent) thought their advanced degree was worth the cost.

Using data from the Gallup poll, researchers found that the financial strain caused by debt *lowered* people's sense of well-being. "Low levels of debt are common and can be used for instrumental purposes of purchasing necessities such as a car," the researchers wrote in a 2016 study published in the *Journal of Happiness Studies*. "By contrast, inordinate levels of debt that are not manageable can consume one's life and attention. Being in deep debt leads to stresses during regular loan repayments and in daily life."

I counseled someone who was enrolled in a health-care executive MBA program that was going to cost $75,000. He was paying for the program with student loans. He wanted to use the MBA degree to open the door to a different career and a federal job. He and his wife were already in debt from credit cards and other loans for about $43,000. I asked him one question: "How do you know the degree will help you get the job you want in the new career field?" The graduate school recruiters had told him so, he said. "Did you talk to anyone other than the school officials about how the MBA would help you get a job?" I asked. "No," he simply said. "Did you talk to professionals in the field who could give you advice on how an advanced degree could help?" I followed up. Again he said, "No."

I encouraged him to drop out of the program and do more research before amassing $75,000 in debt. He listened to my advice. When he dropped out, his professors did everything to convince him to stay. His classmates were shocked. Yet several of them shared that they too were worried about the debt they would have at the end of the program and admired his courage in stopping to rethink his plan.

Less than a year later, he had found the federal job he wanted, paying about $65,000. His income eventually jumped to six figures, no executive MBA needed.

This man and his wife said they are living their best life ever. And because they aren't saddled with student loans, they have been able to provide financial support to friends and family in need. "I think it's important to stress that we stepped out on faith," the couple wrote to me when I asked in retrospect if they regretted following my advice. "We went against the grain. The road wasn't easy, but we knew after talking to you that we couldn't afford any more debt."

You should read "Is College Still Worth It? The New Calculus of Falling Returns," a 2019 article published in the *Fed-*

eral Reserve Bank of St. Louis Review. "Signs have emerged that the economic benefits of college may be diminishing," the authors write. "Despite large income and wealth advantages enjoyed on average by families with a head with a bachelor's degree or higher over families with a head without a postsecondary degree, recent cohorts of college graduates appear to be faring less well than previous generations."

It's not that a college education doesn't boost income. It does, on average. But as the Fed paper points out, the premium of a higher degree is diminishing for some people, particularly minorities, who tend to take on more debt to complete their degrees.

Before amassing a lot of student loan debt or paying for job training at some sketchy, for-profit college, do some real legwork. Talk to folks in the field and find out if you actually need the degree.

At CareerOneStop.org, a site sponsored by the Labor Department, you'll find sections on how to explore various careers, including the "mySkills myFuture" website, where you can find new career options based on the skills and experience you've gained from a previous job. You just enter a past skill or job and the system matches you with similar careers. The site includes job listings, typical salary ranges, and education requirements. You can also narrow your search by location.

I put in "journalist" and was matched with editing and public relations positions. There was also a listing for intelligence analysts. And that makes sense. As a journalist, I am trained to gather, analyze, and evaluate information from a variety of sources. The match posted more than 1,200 job listings, including some that provided training. The typical salaries ranged from $58,900 to $107,000 when I searched the database.

If you think you need to upgrade your skills, check out lo-cal community colleges for certificate programs. Look for job-training grants in your state that may even pay for com-munity college classes. The U.S. Department of Labor's Trade Adjustment Assistance Community College and Career Training program has offered grants to help the unemployed train and find work in certain in-demand industries. In 2011, the Obama administration issued $500 million in grants to community colleges for training and workforce development to help dislocated workers change careers. At the time, Jill Biden, a community college professor, championed the pro-gram. Close to 300 schools received grants.

The bottom line: Don't commit to taking on student loans before doing some research first. You may find that you can get training for the next job without the debt.

I've been laid off. Should I put my student loans in forbearance?

If you have a federally backed loan, forbearance is an option that allows you to temporarily suspend your student loan payments. But be aware that interest will still accrue, mak-ing your balance grow (although during the COVID-19 crisis, Congress automatically suspended interest, payments, and involuntary collection for most people with federal student loans).

Millions of borrowers were not eligible for the 2020 pay-ment reprieve because their federal loans are held by private companies. Nonetheless, many private lenders allowed peo-ple to postpone their payments, although the interest still ac-crued.

It's better to ask for a forbearance, even if your loan will in-

crease, than to default on the debt. But don't make forbearance your first option. If you aren't already in an income-
driven repayment plan, look for one, which will base your
monthly loan payments on your income and family size. For
information about the different income-driven plans, check
with your loan servicer. You can also go to studentaid.gov and
use the loan simulator to help decide which repayment plan
works best for you.

Under ordinary circumstances I would encourage you to
try to keep up with your debt payments. But don't stress yourself out if you have only enough money coming in to cover basic necessities. Once things improve financially, you can make
extra payments to put yourself back on the road to getting rid
of the debt.

Because of a downturn in the economy, my company is suspending the company 401(k) match. What should I do?

During the Great Recession of 2008–2009, many companies
canceled their matching contributions, but most resumed
them once the crisis was over and the economy started to recover. Many reinstated their 401(k) match within a year of
suspending it. Fidelity Investments, one of the country's largest retirement-plan providers, polled about 1,000 employers
at the start of the coronavirus pandemic and found that most
companies hadn't planned to suspend or reduce their company match.

If you can, you should contribute at least enough to your
401(k) account or similar workplace plan to get the maximum
match by your company. In 2020, the most popular formula
was a 100 percent match for the first 3 percent of employee

contributions and then a 50 percent match for the next 2 percent. About 40 percent of 401(k) plans use this formula, according to Fidelity.

Clearly, a company match is free money. The end of this benefit can be extremely disappointing. The nonpartisan Employee Benefit Research Institute and Greenwald & Associates found in a 2017 survey that 73 percent of workers who weren't investing for retirement said they would likely save if contributions were matched by their employer.

Let's say you're earning $50,000 a year and you contribute 3 percent of your pay, or $125, every month to your retirement plan. If your employer matches your contributions at 100 percent up to 3 percent, that's another $125, for a total contribution of $250 a month. Now let's see how much that match is worth. Assuming a 10 percent return over 20 years, the retirement fund could grow to a total balance of $94,916, including the $30,000 the company contributed to your 401(k).

That's a lot of money gone missing from your retirement account if your company ends the match. Still, don't let the absence of a match keep you from saving. It's a nice bonus to have a company match, but with or without the contributions, you still need to save and invest for yourself.

If I lose my job because of a layoff, should I take Social Security early?

Fifty-seven percent of all retirees rely on Social Security as their primary source of income, according to a 2018 Gallup poll.

Generally, many financial experts say you should wait until you're 70 to collect Social Security to maximize your benefits. There's a huge financial incentive to waiting. If you claim your

Social Security early, at 62, rather than waiting until your full retirement age, your monthly benefit drops by as much as 30 percent. However, every year you delay beyond your full retirement age, up to age 70, you get an 8 percent increase in your benefit. There is no point in waiting past age 70 to start receiving Social Security, because benefits stop growing at that point.

My husband and I have long discussed the Social Security question: Do we take our benefits early, or do we wait? We both reach our full retirement age when we turn 67. My husband created a spreadsheet to determine how long it would take us to break even: to catch up on all the cash we missed out on by not collecting early, at 62. His figures showed we would break even around age 79.

The decision to start to collect Social Security early should be done only after you ask yourself this important question: Can I wait to take the money so my benefits can grow? Don't make a quick decision, especially if it's possible you may return to work. If you return to work, even part-time, consider how the income will affect your Social Security benefit.

You can work and still collect Social Security. But if you haven't reached your full retirement age, your benefits are reduced by $1 for every $2 you earn above the annual limit. Starting with the month you reach your full retirement age, your benefits won't be subject to the offset, no matter how much you earn.

Social Security considers the wages you make from a job or your net earnings if you're self-employed. Income from annuities, investment income, pensions, interest, capital gains, and government benefits *do not* count.

The Social Security Administration provides this example of the work offset using the 2021 earnings limit. Let's say that you file for Social Security benefits at age 62 in January 2021, and your payment will be $600 per month ($7,200 for the year). You plan to work during the year and will earn $23,920, which is $4,960 above the 2021 annual earning limit of $18,960. The SSA will withhold $2,480 of your Social Security benefits ($1 for every $2 you earn over the limit). To do this, the agency will withhold your payments from January through May. Beginning in June 2021, you will receive your $600 benefit, and this amount will be paid to you each month for the remainder of the year.

I can understand if this seems confusing. It's not just you. My head hurts too. To figure out how this rule might affect you, go to ssa.gov and search for and read "How Work Affects Your Benefits." You'll also find calculators on the website to help you estimate your payments, which you should do to help in the decision of when to apply for Social Security benefits.

With the reduction in benefits, if you're earning too much, it's better to wait to collect your Social Security. But circumstances can change. Life may make the choice for you. If an economic catastrophe is making it hard for you to pay your bills, you have to do what you need to do. You may not be able to afford to wait until your full retirement age or until you reach 70 to maximize your benefits. And that's okay. It is what it is. The reality is that you may not be able to wait to collect Social Security because you need the money now. Health should also play into the decision about when to claim your benefits.

I've been laid off. I want to start my own business. Is this a good idea?

I'm a woman of faith, and there's an expression I hear all the time from the older church attendees: "When God closes one door, He opens another." As hard a hit as it may be, the loss of your job can be an opportunity to pivot to something you've always wanted to do. Many workers who were laid off during the 2008–2009 financial crisis started their own businesses. "The rate of transition into self-employment did in fact increase during the Great Recession," according to a 2011 report from the Federal Reserve Bank of Cleveland. Nonetheless, the report went on to say, "Transition into self-employment is only part of the story. Many people who were self-employed before the recession exited during the downturn. Despite the claim that recessions are a time of opportunity for entrepreneurs, the Great Recession had a negative impact on U.S. entrepreneurship. At the end of the recession, the United States had fewer businesses and self-employed people than it had before the downturn began."

That's the bad news. It's hard for businesses, especially start-ups, to succeed during an economic downturn. Still, with the right business plan and enough capital, you may find a niche to make a go of it. "During periods of economic decline, whether widespread or cyclical for a particular type of business, entrepreneurs are most likely to bear the brunt," the U.S. Small Business Administration says. "Yet the fact that conditions are changing opens up opportunities for resourceful firms to outsmart larger competitors who, during a downturn, carry on business as usual or are unable to adapt quickly — except to fire employees."

Before committing to being an entrepreneur, do your homework. I mean it. As talented as you may be and no matter how good your business idea is, you need a comprehensive plan, a budget, and a good tax person. Also, ask for help. I suggest you visit the Small Business Administration's website, sba.gov. The SBA's Small Business Development Centers program can provide assistance. Check out Kauffman FastTrac at fasttrac.org, which is part of the Ewing Marion Kauffman Foundation, a nonpartisan foundation that supports entrepreneurship. Find out if your state has a small business development center. Look for help at the local community college.

The key is to dream big, but not so big that you aren't realistic. It may take time for you to make money, so how will you cover your expenses while you're trying to build your business? Watch the debt. Manage your expenses. And for goodness' sake, if you can't make a profit after years of trying, maybe what you have is really a hobby and not a sustainable business enterprise.

Instead of abandoning working for someone, you can always pursue your entrepreneurial passions part-time or through a side gig. I'm a big believer in multiple streams of income. Be sure to check the section in the book about side gigs for more information.

CONSUMER BUYING ISSUES DURING AN ECONOMIC CRISIS

The auto shop at the dealership gave me a hefty repair estimate and I don't have the money to fix my car. The dealership is offering to finance a new car. Should I get my car repaired or take out a loan for a new car?

I have some questions for you: Did you do the math? Which costs less in the end, your car repair or a new car? Too often the decision to buy a new car is made at the repair shop, and that's a mistake. It's the wrong place and time to make this kind of decision.

One of the questions I get asked most frequently is about

an expensive car repair. People want a rule of thumb for when it's time to replace a car.

Let me tell you a story. After church service one day, a fellow parishioner came up to me. She had been talked into buying a new car. She had taken her car to the dealership for service and was told that she needed about $8,000 in repairs. Conveniently, a salesman was right there to persuade her to upgrade. Except here was the problem: She was upside-down on her current car, meaning that she owed more on the auto loan than the vehicle was worth. By the way, the vehicle was only about five years old. No problem, the salesman told her. He could put her into a new $30,000 car, and he advised her to let the previous lender repossess the old car. After preparing all the paperwork, the dealership let her take the new car home for the weekend to think about it.

When the parishioner told me this story, I advised her to take the car back immediately, and she did. I gave her the name of my mechanic, who priced out the repairs she actually needed. The cost of the repairs in the end was only $700.

When it comes to an older car, especially one that still runs well (once repaired, of course), consider all the costs versus purchasing a new vehicle or even a newer used car—dealer fees, taxes, tags, higher insurance premiums, and interest if you get a loan. By the way, the average auto loan is six years. In most cases you will find that it's still less expensive to repair your old car and keep driving it.

There's also the devil you know. If you can't afford a new car and need to buy a used one, you don't really know what you're getting, even if it's been "certified" to be in good condition. At least with your old car you are fully aware of all its issues.

Of course, there are other reasons besides constant repairs that may have you wanting to trade up to a new or newer used car. Perhaps you want newer safety features. Even if you can afford the repairs, you may find that the breakdowns are becoming too frequent and often leave you stranded. The stress and worry that your car might not start is a good reason to shop for a replacement.

The one thing you shouldn't do is make the decision on whether to junk your clunker while standing in the repair shop. You'll be too emotional. And there are too many shiny new cars around to tempt you. If you can, call for a ride home and then do some research before you buy.

I've seen advice saying that if the cost of repairs exceeds the vehicle's market value or adds up to more than a year's worth of auto loan payments, it may be time to ditch the car. This rule of thumb could work as a starting point to consider your choices. You may also want to develop your own rule of thumb for a car replacement. One reader told me that he decides to get rid of a car when the annual repair expenses exceed 50 percent of the cost of a year's worth of new car payments.

My rule is to replace the vehicle if it strands me three times with no indication whatsoever that a repair was necessary. I should add, however, that I have not had a car loan for more than 20 years. The last time I had a car loan, after I paid it off I kept making the monthly payments to myself, so that when I actually need to replace my car, I have the cash to pay for it. This is doable if you keep and maintain your car for 10 or 15 years.

One site to visit as you contemplate the dilemma of repairing a car versus buying a new car is Edmunds.com, an online automotive advice, news, and review site. Read the site's articles on the repair-versus-replace debate. "Buying a new car might seem like the easy way out of a high repair bill, but depending on your circumstances, it may not be the best financial decision," Edmunds says. As part of your decision-making process, also use Edmunds's True Cost to Own Calculator.

Clearly, there are pros and cons to keeping your car and making the repairs. Buying new will make you feel more secure and perhaps safer, but then you may have added debt to your budget at a time when your finances are tight.

Whatever you decide, don't make the decision under duress. Think it through. Sure, a $1,200 car repair bill can be upsetting, especially if you don't have the cash. But don't make a short-term decision (buying a new car because of a high repair bill) without weighing the long-term consequences (more debt).

I can't afford to buy a car. Should I lease?

I have never recommended that someone lease a car. Never. I think leasing, in which at the end of the agreement you do not have ownership of the vehicle, is foolhardy.

Often people lease so that they can drive a car they can't afford to buy. Or, they are focused on the monthly payment alone — again so they can drive a car that's out of their league financially. Sure, leasing can have lower costs during the three-year contract. But as the expression goes, that's penny wise, pound foolish, which means that you are focused on the short term and ignoring the longer-term costs.

I understand the appeal of leasing. The monthly payments can typically be less than loan payments on a new car. You can drive a late-model car. You don't want to worry about maintenance costs. If you're running a business and use the car for your enterprise, there is a nice tax break. (Although it's not as generous as some people think. Often business owners will brag that they can take a deduction for all the expenses for the lease, even though the car is not exclusively used for their business. Only the business-related portion of the lease payment is deductible, the IRS says.)

I talked to an expert at Edmunds.com, and he was more forgiving of people who want to lease. If you are a repeat leaser, you are going to spend more money over time. "The smartest people I know make the worst financial decisions," said Ivan Drury, senior manager, Insights, at Edmunds. "Leasing definitely has its place – if you don't drive a lot of miles and you want a nicer car."

I see more downside than upside to leasing.

- It can trap you into a cycle of lease payments in which you never own a car outright.
- You have to pay extra at the end of the lease for going over the mileage limit. This may cost you anywhere from 10 cents to 20 cents for each mile over the limit. Most leases allow for annual limits between 10,000 to 15,000 miles.
- You could end up with expensive charges for excessive wear and tear.
- There are early-termination fees.

Overall, buying a car and keeping it for years after you pay off the loan is far cheaper than leasing. If you pay for the car with cash, even better.

And buying a new or used car has never been easier. There are so many websites to help you figure out the right vehicle at the right price to fit your budget. Here are a few I use when I want to buy a car:

- Edmunds.com
- KBB.com
- CarGurus.com
- ConsumerReports.com

If you are short of cash, leasing is an easier way than buying to get into a new car. But I want to get you to look beyond your current situation and economic crisis. One of the reasons you can't get ahead financially is that you don't consider the long-term costs of the decisions you make.

Buy, don't lease. Manage your expectations and opt for an affordable used car or new car. Check online for the latest list of the "most reliable used cars." Search for that term and you'll find a list of cars under $10,000 and even $5,000. For now, you might just have a Kia or Chevrolet budget, and that's okay.

I keep overspending at the grocery store, because food is a necessity. But with times being tight, I have to cut back. How do I do that?

I find that a lot of people overspend at the grocery store, and it's easy to see why. Of course food is essential. And you shop when you're hungry. (Never go grocery shopping when you are starving!) The challenge is to treat what you spend on food like any other expense category: Set a budget and then stick to it.

A survey by LendingTree found that nearly a third of respondents (31 percent) say they "almost always" overspend at the grocery store. Men are twice as likely as women to exceed their food budget. During a crisis, people tend to panic-shop. The coronavirus pushed people's spending up at the supermarket. "Whether it's due to having more family members at home for every meal or because consumers tend to panic-shop and stock up in times of crisis, the pandemic has definitely brought with it increased grocery spending, costing households around $100 more a month than before the spread of the coronavirus," LendingTree found. Nearly a third of Americans almost always overspend on groceries despite using shopping lists and coupons, according to the survey.

I've found that these tips work for many people:

- **Push back from plastic.** Don't use a debit or credit card. Instead, shop with cash. Studies show that consumers tend to spend more when they use plastic — debit or credit — than cash. "What? Wait, why give up my debit card?" you might protest. "I can't spend more than what's in my account with a debit card," you would probably argue. Oh, but you can overspend your budget using your debit card. Let's say you have $100 in your checking account. You head to the store to buy just milk, eggs, and bread. That's all that's on your list. In fact, you really can't afford to spend more. You're on a strict budget because things are tight financially. But with the debit card you can overspend, because you have at least $100 in your account. In contrast, if you have only $15 in cash, that's all you can really spend.
- **Eat what you have at home.** Unless you need perishables, don't go back to the grocery store until you've consumed all the extra food you have in your house. Yes, dig out that frozen chicken from the back of the freezer. Figure out a good bean stew with all the cans of beans you've been collecting. For some this won't be a hard task, since there isn't much extra. But for others there is.
- **Pretend you're on Food Network's *Chopped*.** Google it.

It's one of my favorite television shows. Chefs are given a basket of ingredients and must plan a meal using four random items. Get creative with the food you already have. In a browser, just type in the items and see what comes up. I've made some of my best meals using what I already had in the house. Okay, there were a few misses, but I've saved money by keeping my family's food budget in check.

If I buy one and get a second one for half off the price, doesn't it make sense to get the second one, even if I don't need it right now?

Discounts make us dumb. You may be so focused on snagging a sale that you don't consider the fact that you aren't really saving any money.

Repeat after me: "I never save when I spend." Now let me say it for you. *You never save when you spend.*

If you don't understand what I mean, let me explain. Let's say you purchase a $100 coat on sale, with the store advertising that the coat is 50 percent off the original price. You think you've saved $100. But you haven't saved that money. You've spent $100. Unless you rush right to the bank and put $100 in your emergency fund, you have not engaged in the act of saving. You're just a spender who spent less.

It's important that you understand this concept so that you stop and really think about whether your so-called bargain shopping is increasing your wealth. If your plan was to buy one pair of shoes but you come home with two, what have you accomplished? You had planned to spend money for only one pair of shoes. Retailers know that Americans love bargains.

You're feeling pleased with yourself that you beat the system. Yet you went over budget, even at half off.

One of my all-time favorite books, which I keep right next to my desk to pull out whenever someone is crowing about how much they saved while shopping, is *Dollars and Sense: How We Misthink Money and How to Spend Smarter*, by Dan Ariely and Jeff Kreisler. "When we see a sale, we shouldn't consider what the price used to be or how much we're spending," the authors write. "Rather we should consider what we're actually going to spend. Buying a $60 shirt marked down from $100 isn't 'saving $40.' It is spending $60."

Think of the opportunity costs when you spend. What if you lost your job? The money you spent on that extra pair of shoes could pay a utility bill later, during a financial crisis. "The way we should think about the opportunity costs of money is that when we spend money on one thing, it's money that we cannot spend on something else, neither right now nor anytime later," according to Ariely and Kreisler.

It's not that you shouldn't take advantage of a discount or even use coupons. When you buy something that you need and the cost is within your budget, discounts help you spend less. Just keep in mind that a sale only invites you to spend, not save.

I can get a new TV for no money down and no interest for 12 months. What a deal! I should go for it, right?
Be very careful of no-interest financing. These deals may be promoted as "deferred-interest plans" where there's no interest for 12 or 18 months. But be aware that this is credit with a catch. The no-interest deals typically involve applying for a

credit card. You just have to pay the balance in full by the end of the promotional period.

Retailers use such promotions to entice consumers to purchase big-ticket items, such as a television, refrigerator, or furniture. Medical professionals also use the promotions to help patients strapped for cash pay for their care.

Before signing up, just be sure you know the difference between zero-interest and deferred-interest promotions.

Zero percent interest. You pay interest only on whatever remaining balance you have, starting with the date the promotional period ends. You will probably need to make minimum monthly payments on time throughout the length of the offer.

Let's say you purchased a big-screen television for $2,500. During the promotion you lose your job, or your side-gig income is reduced. You've managed to pay off half of the $2,500. The interest then starts to kick in, but you are charged interest only on the remaining $1,250 balance.

Deferred interest. If you don't pay off the entire balance by the end of the promotion, you'll be charged interest going back to the original date of the purchase.

Using the TV example, under a deferred-interest promotion, you made just the minimum payments. Those amounts were deducted from what you owe; however, the interest charged on the balance was left to accrue. All the interest charged but not collected becomes due if you don't pay off the entire balance by the time the promotion ends. The interest is then added to the amount you still owe on your purchase.

The math could work out like the following, according to the National Consumer Law Center. You buy the $2,500 television in November using a one-year, 24 percent deferred-interest plan. You pay off all but $100 by the following November. But the lender adds nearly $400 in interest on the entire $2,500, dating back one year, to the next bill.

"Deferred-interest promotions are one of the biggest credit card traps on the market today," stated National Consumer Law Center staff attorney Chi Chi Wu, who authored a report on the hidden time bomb of deferred-interest credit cards. "Avoid them at all costs. 'No interest' sounds tempting now, but you could end up in the trap of huge interest payments later." Deferred-interest credit cards typically carry very high interest rates, with an average of 24 percent and as high as 29.99 percent.

The law center noted that a Consumer Financial Protection Bureau study found that for consumers with low credit scores, who are likely to be financially vulnerable, more than 40 percent were not able to pay off the balance by the end of the deferred-interest period. "Better-off consumers get the benefit of interest-free financing, while credit card lenders make their profits off of financially constrained consumers," the law center pointed out.

The National Consumer Law Center highlighted this real complaint submitted to the Consumer Financial Protection Bureau:

I was told that I should apply for a credit card by my surgery facility in order to pay for my surgery and that many patients have done it before and are happy with the decision. My surgery was in the summer of 2013 and cost $3,000 but now since it is past the promotional period that I was not made aware of, the interest I pay on it monthly is 26%. That is insanely high

in my opinion . . . I feel like I was fooled into believing
that this would help me pay for surgery, yet it has cost
me so much more money than I can afford. I'm a college
student and can barely make it financially as is, but to
have this kind of financial stress on me every month is
too much. 26% interest is a crime!

If consumers stop buying, won't the U.S. economy tank?
Your main concern should be what's happening in your own
household. Don't shop to save America. Save to protect your
family's financial future.

Whenever I argue that people need to save more, someone
always emails me to say I'm going to tank the economy with
all my talk about how people should stop overspending. Let
the Federal Reserve worry about the U.S. economy. Your focus
should be on your own economic well-being.

FAMILY MONEY MATTERS

My daughter and her boyfriend can't pay their rent.
   Should I help them out even if it means I can't cover
   my own rent?
My question to you: Where would you live if you got kicked
out of your own home? Never give what you can't afford. Give
out of your abundance, because you should take care of your
needs first. Worst case, your daughter comes back home – mi-
nus the boyfriend who isn't working.

In looking at the economic well-being of U.S. households,
the Federal Reserve repeatedly finds that many adults are not
well prepared to withstand even small financial disruptions.

Unexpected expenses, such as repairing a car, replacing a broken appliance, or incurring a modest medical expense, can be a hardship for families without adequate savings.

When faced with a hypothetical expense of $400, 63 percent of adults said in 2019 that they would cover the expense using cash, savings, or a credit card paid off at the next statement, according to the Fed. But that was only 63 percent of all families. That leaves a lot of people unable to come up with $400 for an emergency. "For these adults, the most common approach was to pay for the expense using a credit card and then carry a balance," the Fed reported.

So yes, if you are in a position to help a family member or friend, you should. Refer to my recommendations earlier in the book on helping friends and family.

My mother is a spendthrift and is constantly asking me for money. But shouldn't I continue to help her? She's my mother, after all.

See my previous answer, because the advice doesn't change just because the person in need is your mama. Certainly you want to make sure your parents have the basic necessities, but beyond that, you may have to step back and let the natural consequences of their actions break their spendthrift habits. Besides, coming to someone's rescue all the time could jeopardize your financial safety.

Let me use the example of a lifeguard. All three of my children are certified lifeguards. One of the things they learn in their safety training is how to help someone who is drowning or in distress without letting that person pull them under too. A drowning person who is flailing about, desperate and scared, can drown you as you try to pull him to safety. A trained lifeguard will toss the person a lifesaving device, such as a rescue tube or a rope line.

A financially distressed person can panic and reach for your help too. But if you're not careful, you might also succumb. You want to practice the same caution as a lifeguard.

Help your mother, friend, or relative, but not in a way that will jeopardize your financial safety. Throw the person a line by helping her find resources to manage her money better. Have her contact the National Foundation for Credit Counseling, which is the organization of nonprofit financial counseling agencies. NFCC-affiliated organizations offer low-cost debt counseling and debt management plans. You can find more information at nfcc.org.

Should I cosign?

Far too often people think that by cosigning you are the backup borrower. Nope. You are on the hook from the jump. A CreditCards.com survey found that 38 percent of cosigners had to pay some or all of the loan or credit card bill because the primary borrower did not. The survey also found that 28 percent of cosigners experienced a drop in their credit scores because the primary borrower paid late or not at all. In fact, lenders can come after you right away. They are going to look for the person with the better potential to pay.

There are some other effects on your credit history when you cosign.

- If collection actions are pursued, you could end up paying late fees and even be subject to a wage garnishment.

- Any late payments by the primary borrower will show up on your credit report.
- Cosigning limits your ability to borrow. The debt becomes part of your credit history. So if you cosign for a car for someone and find you need a car loan, you may not be approved, or you may be charged a higher interest rate because your credit report indicates you are obligated to a lot of debt.
- Life happens. An unexpected economic downturn can quickly turn a good money manager into a struggling debtor.

But I get it. You may still want to help a child, friend, or family member. If so, do the following:

- Get intimate with the person's budget. Look at the numbers yourself. Can he or she really afford the loan?
- If you do cosign, you'd better be able to make the payment if the primary borrower can't for any reason. Seriously, this has to be possible, or you may find yourself in financial trouble.
- Make sure you are getting the monthly loan statements/bills too. You don't want a nasty surprise that the loan is six months past due.
- Be prepared to pitch in with a payment if the person runs into financial trouble. To save your credit, be advised: You may have to pick up the payments for a few months or longer.

One last caution. If you're going to cosign, consider this fact from a CreditCards.com survey: 26 percent of cosigners said their relationship with the primary signer was ruined after cosigning.

My child has graduated from college but can't find a job. Should I let her move back home?

Many young adults have boomeranged back home because they can't find a job in a bad economy. Stagnant wages and overwhelming student loans can bring your child back to the nest, and I'm not opposed to such an arrangement. It's hard out there, especially if your child is a recent graduate.

The coronavirus pandemic pushed millions of Americans, especially young adults, to move back in with family members, according to the Pew Research Center. Several months into the spread of COVID-19 in the U.S., 52 percent of young adults were living with one or both of their parents.

So yes, you should let your kid come home to save or pay off debt. I'm on a mission to get young adults to stay home into their late twenties or even early thirties. Rather than a sign that they've failed to set out on their own, I see it as an opportunity for them to save aggressively so that when they do leave, they will have a substantial emergency fund. Or they should stay long enough to pay off their student loans.

A lot of young adults are stressed out and overwhelmed by the cost of living on their own. Allowing them a break from the expenses of adulthood isn't enabling them if you do it right. You're just giving them some financial breathing room.

We should remove the stigma that young adults returning home is embarrassing or a sign that they are financial failures. They are not, especially if you allowed or encouraged your child to attend a college that necessitated some heavy borrowing.

The move back should be done in a way that will help your child eventually become independent. Here's what I recommend.

Establish a timeline. If the primary reason for moving back home is to pay off debt, make sure your young adult has an aggressive plan to get rid of the debt. Bankrate.com has a calculator that shows the impact of accelerating debt payments.

Do regular budget checkups. Verify that your child is sticking to the debt or savings plan. If she returned home just to save, make sure that's happening.

Don't be a pushover parent. If your child is overspending, call him on it. Don't be oppressively hard on him in terms of having some fun, but make sure it's within reason. If you're feeling that he is having too much fun while you're paying for food, utilities, and so forth, then the plan you agreed to when he moved back isn't working and it may be time for him to go.

My adult child needs to move back home to save money [or get out of debt]. Should I charge rent?

Don't require rent if you don't need the money. The point of the move back home is to allow your child to take as much of his or her income — and it should be a significant percentage — as needed to save or get out of debt as quickly as possible.

I expect I'll get some pushback on this answer. When I made this recommendation in my *Washington Post* column, I received quite a bit of email from parents who disagreed. "On the contrary, charging some rent, even if below-market, provides a transition into the real world," one reader wrote.

I'm not a rookie. I have three children, and at the time of this book's publication they were all in their early twenties.

My husband and I offered them all the opportunity to live at home and save. (We had saved enough to send them to college without any debt.)

We think of it this way. Let's say your adult child had a net income of $34,000 when starting out. Allowing for some personal expenses, car insurance, and other costs during the year, she could save $20,000 a year by not paying rent. In five years, she could save well over $100,000 (and that's not counting any salary increases). That's a significant down payment on a home or contribution to a retirement fund, which would put her well in the millionaire club by the time she retires. This would be a financial game-changer.

We suggested that our kids stay long enough to be able to pay cash for their first home. Again, can you imagine what it would mean for them to spend most of their adult life with no mortgage or rent payments? That's huge. And in the span of a lifetime, the time they lived at home would be just a blip. What an incredible gift you would be giving your children.

But since the best-laid plans don't always go as planned, I have some recommendations about when you should and shouldn't charge rent.

Coming home with college debt. No rent. They should be allowed to use as much of their income as they can to get out of their debt quickly.

Coming home to save. No rent. Again, this is about freeing your adult child from everyday expenses so that he can stockpile a lot of cash.

Reneging on his plan to pay down a student loan. Charge rent. Start off slow, and if he doesn't get the message, push the rent up to a market rate. One of two things will happen. Your child will say, "If I'm paying this much in rent, I might as well have my own place." *Ding. Ding. Yup, you've got to go.* Or he will wise up and get back on track. Give him a chance to return to the original agreement. But if he relapses, charge rent.

Reneging on a plan to save aggressively. Charge rent. No, she doesn't get to live free and live it up on your dime.

The Future

You have to live in the present, but you also must plan for your future needs. Yet there's a reason that you may not be hardwired to deal with present and future financial issues: It turns out that thinking about important financial decisions not only stresses people out, it affects brain function, according to research by Northwestern Mutual.

Here's the good news and why this section and others in this book can help: When people get help while making financial decisions, their brains tend to relax, concentrate, and make better choices, according to Northwestern Mutual's 2017 Brain on Finance Study. Northwestern Mutual partnered with ThinkAlike Laboratories, a neuroscience research firm, to measure the electrical activity of people's brains when they are evaluating various financial scenarios. Neuroscientists found that receiving guidance affected the brain in three important ways: People paid more attention, they had a stronger ability to understand the crucial concepts they were considering, and they relaxed more. "Put simply, when individuals were guided through the decision-making process, they were 21% less stressed than when they were unassisted," researchers found.

Let me help you. The future can be scary. Your brain wants to shut down because of this. But shutting down or ignoring issues won't make the situation get better or go away.

In this section, I walk through some of the most frequently asked questions about saving and investing for the future.

INVESTING

When and how should I start saving to invest?

For this question and the next one, I consulted Carolyn McClanahan, a certified financial planner. She and I talk often about investing and how people need to create an investing plan so that when a crisis that significantly affects the stock market hits, they don't panic. "People shouldn't invest based on how the market is doing," she says. "They should invest based on their investment policy."

First, let's discuss when you should start investing. The earlier you start, the better, and the sooner you reach the financial independence you probably crave. (She agrees with me that if you have high-cost debt, focus on that first. She also recommends having an emergency fund set aside so you are less likely to tap your investments in the event of a financial emergency.)

If you can, invest in your company's retirement plan, if there is one. At a minimum, invest enough to get any company match. If you're in a low tax bracket, especially if you are young, put money into a Roth IRA. If you are in a higher tax bracket, open a regular IRA, especially if you don't have a workplace retirement plan. You'll have to pay taxes on the withdrawals in the future, but you'll save money on the taxes now.

Now about the how. "The stock market comes to mind

when most people think of investing, and to many the stock market involves taking on a lot of risk. In reality, there are many types of investments," McClanahan points out.

There are individual shares of stocks and mutual funds that own stocks. Stocks have the chance of high return but also significant losses. "Stock shares are issued by large companies, small companies, and international companies. It's good to have a mix of all kinds of stocks," she recommends.

There are bonds, which you buy when you lend a company or government money and they have an obligation to pay you back with interest. "Bonds are not as risky as stocks and consequently don't have high returns," McClanahan explains. "They act as a safety net in a portfolio, especially for a person who is near retirement."

You can invest in real estate or in commodities such as oil or gold. But these are specialized investments and should generally be avoided by people just starting out, she cautions.

"The easiest and smartest way to invest is through index funds," McClanahan says. "These are low-cost funds that invest in a large basket of stocks, bonds, and other types of individual investments."

Your 401(k) plan might offer a mix of funds, and now most offer "target-date" or "life-cycle" funds that allocate your money among various asset classes. These funds automatically shift from riskier investments to more conservative ones as you reach a certain target age, such as retirement. For example, a worker in his thirties who might have 30 to 40 years until retirement would invest in a target-date fund geared toward retirement in 2050 or 2060. This fund might be invested in about 90 percent stocks and 10 percent bonds. The allocation would shift away from stocks and toward more bonds as the investor gets closer to the target retirement date. Think of target-date funds like a set-it-and-forget-it slow cooker in which you're preparing a stew. The idea is that you don't have to monitor your investment account closely because the asset allocation and rebalancing are done for you at the appropriate times.

I'm close to retirement [or retired]. Shouldn't I take my money out of the stock market?

A top financial expert put it so well when I asked him this very question. "Regardless of what happens in the short term, you can't let that derail your long-term financial planning," said Greg McBride, chief financial analyst for Bankrate.com. "The day you retire, it's not like you're going to withdraw all your money that one day. No, it still needs to last you another 25, 30, 35 years. So even then, the day you retire, you have an investment horizon that is still measured in decades."

Consider this from the Social Security Administration as of 2020:

- A man reaching age 65 can expect to live, on average, until 84.
- A woman turning 65 can expect to live, on average, until 86.5.
- About one out of every three 65-year-olds will live past age 90.
- About one out of seven 65-year-olds will live past age 95.

It's very likely you will live a long life, so let some of your money stay invested and grow. But once you are close to retirement or retired, it is important to dial down the risk, although you still need to own some stocks, McClanahan says.

Now let's discuss the need for an investment policy. The way to avoid being worried about the amount of risk you're taking is to develop an investment policy, which might state what percent will be invested in stocks and bonds, she advocates. Having a policy to guide your investments will help you avoid making decisions based on fear.

When your percentages get out of balance, you'll return to your investment policy. For example, if you decide that you want to be invested 70 percent in stocks and 30 percent in bonds and after a year of good stock returns you find that your stock allocation is 75 percent, you should sell enough stocks and buy bonds to restore the allocation you established for yourself. This forces you to sell high when stocks are doing well and buy low when stocks are not doing well," McClanahan says. "Investment policies take the emotions and guesswork out of investing."

Your policy will be your own and based on your risk tolerance. McClanahan suggests that your allocation of bonds should cover at least five years of cash-flow needs. If you are within five years of using your investments for retirement, determine whether you'll have enough money to support your living expenses, she says. "Studies have shown that a serious market downturn early in retirement can totally derail a financial plan."

I'm still too scared to invest. Can't I just put my money into a savings account?

When the Dow Jones Industrial Average, the S&P 500, or any other stock market index experiences hair-raising volatility, many people flee to the safety of bank-deposit accounts. However, savers will be exposed to another major risk—inflation.

Inflation is the general rise in the price of goods and services over time. The annual inflation rate in the U.S. from 2010 to 2019 has ranged from a high of 3.14 percent in 2011 to a low of 0.12 percent in 2015, according to Statista, a leading provider of market and consumer data.

Inflation in the U.S. is calculated using the consumer price index, which measures changes over time in the cost of a basket of goods and services bought by a typical American consumer. Sometimes it is referred to as the cost-of-living index. The U.S. Bureau of Labor Statistics has a consumer price index (CPI) inflation calculator. Go to bls.gov and search for "CPI Inflation Calculator," then try it. For example, the purchasing power of $100 in 1990 equaled $198.45 in 2020, according to the calculator.

You need to be concerned about inflation because you'll want to maintain your standard of living in the future. You'll need to make sure you have enough income or savings and/ or investment assets to afford housing, food, health care, and other goods and services.

In response to the 2008 financial crisis, the Federal Reserve dropped the federal funds rate, and savings yields soon plummeted, falling below 1 percent. The same thing happened after the spread of COVID-19 forced the U.S. economy into a recession. Rates on CDs and money market deposit accounts, which are insured by the Federal Deposit Insurance Corporation, sank to 1 percent or below.

Let me put this in another way. Let's say you put $2,000 into a one-year CD, and the average interest rate is a measly 0.98 percent. If inflation is higher than what you are get-ting on your deposit account, you are actually losing money because of inflation. This means you are apt to have trouble buying the things you will need in the future. In short, your money must at least keep pace with inflation.

If you just can't stomach the stock market, then at the very least shop around for the highest-yield savings for a money market account you can find. Look for a financial institution that may have only an online presence but is still backed by the FDIC. Just keep in mind that although you can't lose your savings with these accounts, your money may lose its pur-chasing power because of rising inflation.

Should I be investing for retirement even if I have debt?

The answer to the question of paying off debt versus saving for retirement depends on your age, the amount of debt, how expensive it is to carry the debt, and whether your employer is offering a match for your retirement contributions. You need to save for the future, but you also need to break the bondage of debt that keeps you from having a secure future. Dragging student loan debt into your retirement will be a strain on your fixed income, whether that's a pension (if you're lucky), Social Security, or savings.

The less debt you have, the longer you can survive in an eco-nomic downturn. Investment returns are not guaranteed and can be very volatile. By paying off your debts early, you reduce what you pay in interest, and that should immediately turn into money in the bank or a retirement account. (Or it should. Once you are out of debt, invest your savings carefully.)

If you're deeply in debt and have a few decades before you retire, I think you should focus on paying down what you owe. This might mean pulling back from retirement savings until your debt payments are gone or are at least manageable.

As with any advice, there are a lot of caveats. In general, these are some ways I look at the question of debt payments versus retirement savings.

In your twenties: If you came out of college with a lot of student loans, focus first on getting rid of the debt. (I also recommend living with parents, as I've said.) The exception is if you work for a company that matches your retirement savings. If this is the case, invest enough in your 401(k) to receive the company match. Otherwise, you are leaving money on the table. But beyond getting the match, aggressively pay off your student loans. All of them.

If you are fortunate enough to qualify for the federal government's Public Service Loan Forgiveness Program (PSLF), you can aggressively save for retirement. Under this program, the remaining balance of a borrower's debt is forgiven after 120 qualifying monthly payments. Just be aware that you have to continue working for an eligible employer for the entire time. Only federal direct loans are eligible for PSLF. Also, you must be paying off the debt under a certain type of income-driven repayment plan while working full-time for a qualifying employer. Go to studentaid.gov to be sure you understand and are complying with all the rules.

Now, I know my advice might seem to be contrary to common wisdom, which is that the earlier you start investing, the less you need to invest overall and the higher your returns will be, because you have time on your side. I'd rather you focus on one thing – getting out of debt, which will lay the foundation for you to catch up on saving and investing for retirement once you are debt-free.

The type of debt matters too, but not so much at this age. Often people are told to get rid of any high-interest debt first, such as credit card debt. Student loans with a relatively lower rate don't need to be a priority, you've probably heard.

But there's a problem with this line of thinking. Because student loans are considered "good debt," borrowers often don't see the urgency in getting rid of it. So they get deferments after deferments. A deferment allows borrowers to stop making loan payments if they meet certain criteria, such as economic hardship. Lenders may also grant a forbearance that gives borrowers permission to stop making payments for a set period. But forbearance is generally a more expensive option than deferment, because interest continues to accrue.

Life happens quicker than you think — marriage, kids, mortgage — and with every life event there's another chance you could be forced to start making just the minimum payment on your debts and carrying that burden for more years. Get a head start by getting rid of it as soon as you can.

In your thirties: Follow the advice for a twentysomething, even to the point of living at home or with multiple roommates to get that debt gone (here I'm primarily referring to student loans, credit cards, and personal loans). Retirement savings is a long game.

Remember, when you are in your thirties, you still have at least three decades to save for retirement. Spend this decade becoming debt-free. Again, if your company has a retirement plan match, put in enough to get the matching funds. Stop there, and put the rest of the money you would have used for retirement toward paying off your debt.

However, if you have enough room in your budget to do both — save for retirement and aggressively pay off your debts — then go for it.

In your forties: It's getting close to crunch time to make sure you have adequate retirement savings. By now you may have children. You might be married or have other family obligations, such as taking care of aging parents. Or you have a mortgage and a lifestyle with expenses you just can't see how to reduce.

Get the debt off your books, or you'll be paying off student loans and credit card debt in the crucial years you need to be saving for your retirement.

In your fifties: You are getting very close to a time when you may want to retire or be forced to leave the workforce because of an illness or downsizing, which often happens to older workers, especially during a financial crisis. You'll have to figure out how to get rid of debt and save for your retirement. This may mean some deep, deep cuts to your budget. If you can't cut any more, perhaps you can work another job, get a gig, or start a small business to bring in extra cash.

Don't get discouraged if you're down to the bare bones in your budget and the debt is still dragging you down. Just pace the debt payoff based on when you are able to make extra payments. If the debt is overwhelming, pull back on the retirement savings just a bit and apply money to the debt.

In your sixties and beyond: If you are still working and you are at your highest earning potential, sweep away that debt as soon as possible. If you can make extra debt payments, do so and aggressively save for retirement. If the debt is crushing, you may need to seek advice on filing for bankruptcy protection. (See the FAQ on filing for bankruptcy protection.)

Should I keep investing for retirement if my company is indicating that it may have layoffs?

When faced with a layoff, it's time to go into crisis mode. Comb for places to cut expenses now! Then take any money you can find from cutting costs and save it — *all of it.*

Forget about any plan to aggressively pay off debt. Make the minimum payments on your debts and preserve your cash — unless you already have a very fat emergency fund. If you're set with emergency and short-term savings, then continue to save for retirement. If you stay unemployed longer than you plan for or your money starts to run out, you can always take a hardship withdrawal from your 401(k), 403(b), or other workplace retirement account.

If your rainy-day fund is nonexistent or super-low, suspend contributions to your retirement plan when you're pretty sure you will be laid off or even furloughed. If you lose your job but quickly find another one, you can immediately boost your retirement investing. However, if you spend weeks without a paycheck, you are going to need the cash.

Should I invest in gold and silver when the stock market is tumbling?

Whenever there's an economic downturn and the stock market experiences significant losses, there's often a "gold rush." Investors get nervous and race to buy gold, which is seen as a safe haven when stocks are falling or when inflation is rising. Or, there's a run to purchase silver. Investors are told that investing in gold or silver is a prudent move to hedge against economic uncertainties. But the price of precious metals can experience some major peaks and valleys.

Between 2008 and 2012, the value of gold increased dramatically, the U.S. Bureau of Labor Statistics pointed out in a 2013 report. From September 2010 to September 2011, gold prices increased 50.6 percent because of an uneven recovery from the housing crisis that shook the U.S. financial markets. Gold reached an all-time high of $1,917.90 an ounce in late August 2011.

In fact, investors chasing what they believe is a secure investment can create a gold bubble. "During a bubble, assets typically trade at a price, or within a price range, that greatly exceeds the asset's intrinsic value," says Investopedia.com, a website I highly recommend you bookmark and visit regularly. It's one of the best sites to explain investing and financial terms.

As COVID-19 spread in the U.S., investors again fled to gold, pushing it to another high of nearly $2,000 an ounce. By the end of July 2020, gold was up 27 percent, according to the World Gold Council. People's rush to gold came after a heart-stopping plunge in stocks that began in March 2020. For example, the S&P 500 dropped by 35 percent as the coronavirus began to spread wildly.

A look to the past is a good indicator of what could happen in the future. Over a two-year period during the 1980s, the price of gold plummeted about 65 percent. After gold reached $850 an ounce in January 1980, it would be another 28 years, until January 2008, before investors who bought at the $850 price per ounce broke even. In 2008 gold lost more than 30 percent of its value.

Yes, gold can spike during hard economic times. Yet, pardon the pun, gold isn't always a silver bullet. It comes with risk.

For example, gold loses its luster for investors when the stock market stabilizes. Investors like gold when things are bad, but the appeal of precious metals wanes when things get better. On November 9, 2020, the day when two leading pharmaceutical companies, Pfizer and BioNTech SE, announced that their COVID-19 vaccines were proving very effective, the price of gold dropped about 5 percent, tumbling below $1,900 an ounce.

"An investment in gold is not foolproof," warns the North American Securities Administrators Association. "An investor needs to know his or her investment objectives. Gold may not provide long-term investment returns. Gold is a commodity, and, like other commodities, its price can fluctuate dramatically."

There are a few ways to own gold. You can own physical gold directly or invest in gold-mining companies, gold-related mutual funds, or exchange-traded funds (ETFs) that offer investors exposure to gold. Be careful about any investment promoter who encourages you to have a substantial portion of your portfolio in precious metals. In general, many planners suggest keeping gold or precious metal investment to about 2 percent to 3 percent of your portfolio. "Despite its reputation, gold is not impervious to price declines," warns FINRA, a not-for-profit organization responsible for regulating brokerage firms.

"On balance, gold has a pretty reliable record as a safe haven in times of market turmoil," wrote Amy C. Arnott, a chartered financial analyst and portfolio strategist for Morningstar. "However, it's better viewed as an insurance policy than as a core holding. Investors who decide to add gold to their portfolios should be wary of the current hype surrounding precious metals and be prepared for periodic dry spells."

The bottom line: Yes, gold can be part of your portfolio, but it's important to understand the risk.

REAL ESTATE

If housing prices drop because of an economic downturn, is that the right time to buy?

Yes, take advantage of falling home prices or interest rate drops, but neither of those things should drive the decision to buy a home if you're not ready to become a homeowner. The truth is that for many people homeownership is unaffordable. I recommend you read *100 Questions Every First-Time Home Buyer Should Ask*, by Ilyce R. Glink. "Homeownership is expensive," Glink writes. "It's a big responsibility. It's illiquid (meaning you can't turn around six months later and decide to rent without potentially losing a fair amount of money)."

Bankrate.com found in a 2019 survey that 44 percent of homeowners said they had regrets about their home purchase. For young buyers the number was much higher—63 percent. And what did they regret the most? The Bankrate.com survey found that the most common area of remorse was maintenance, meaning costs that were more expensive than people had expected.

Think ahead. Make up a budget for yourself in homeownership, breaking down all of your projected monthly costs. And when you're finished, go over it again. You don't want any unexpected surprises when you purchase a home.

If mortgage interest rates drop, should I rush to refinance?

It may be a good time for you to refinance, but please run the numbers first. Go to Bankrate.com and use the refinance calculator to figure out if it's worth refinancing.

People are always bragging to me that they refinanced

and didn't have to pay anything. You may not have to put up money at the closing, but your loan definitely cost something. That "no-cost" loan might mean you agreed to roll the cost of the refinance into the loan, which could also mean paying more interest over the life of the loan. When refinancing, you need to take into account those costs and how long you plan to stay in your home.

What if I can't refinance? What should I do?

You may find that you are not able to refinance because you don't qualify for a loan, or because your home is worth less than what you owe, meaning you are underwater. Or maybe you are 15 or 20 years into a 30-year mortgage and you don't want to reset the loan term, essentially starting all over.

Take heart. You can achieve similar results to a mortgage refinance simply by making extra principal payments on your mortgage.

In your Internet browser search for "HSH.com and PreFi prepayment calculator" to figure out how to attain a lower effective mortgage interest rate by prepaying your mortgage principal. The calculator will help if you have a specific dollar amount available for prepayment each month. It calculates your interest savings over the remaining loan term and your effective interest rate as a result of making those extra payments. In short, if you can't refinance your mortgage but you *can* afford to pay some additional money each month, that prepayment might save you as much as an actual refinance. Also known as "paying down your mortgage," this approach is definitely worth considering.

Let's say you are two years into a $200,000, 30-year fixed-rate mortgage at 4.5 percent. You have an extra $200 a month you could apply to the mortgage principal. Without prepayment, you will pay off your loan in 337 months (28.08 years). Total amount of interest you'll pay: $147,819.88. With prepayment of the extra $200 each month, you will pay off your loan in 244 months (20.33 years). Total amount of interest you'll pay: $102,216.80. Your effective interest rate over those 244 months would be 3.843 percent.

Isn't buying a home a good tax break?

Don't buy a home because of the tax break. The fact is that the average homeowner does not even take the mortgage-interest deduction.

The Tax Cuts and Jobs Act increased the standard deduction for taxpayers. The standard deduction for married couples filing jointly for the 2021 tax year is $25,100. For single taxpayers and married individuals filing separately, the standard deduction is $12,550, and for heads of households it's $18,800. The result is that many taxpayers don't itemize, which means they don't benefit from the mortgage-interest deduction.

Prior to the passage of the new tax law, about 30 percent of filers itemized, allowing them to take advantage of the mortgage-interest deduction, according to the Tax Foundation. After the law went into effect, about 10 percent of filers took the deduction.

It's for this same reason that you shouldn't hang on to a mortgage if you can afford to pay it off early.

Even if you do benefit from the mortgage interest deduction, recognize that it's not a credit. A credit reduces your tax burden dollar for dollar. A deduction only reduces the amount of your income subject to taxation.

How much of my income should go toward housing every month?

During the sales presentation for the home my husband and I were building, the real estate agent kept saying, "With your income you can easily afford this house." When we got to the master bathroom, he suggested an upgrade, an expensive Jacuzzi bathtub with water jets. "Oh, that won't add much to your mortgage," he said. Imitating the circling motion of water in such a tub, I said to him, "I can just swish the water around with my hands and save some money."

In my experience, if you're spending more than about 36 percent of your net income on housing (principal, taxes, insurance, homeowners association fees), you'll probably have trouble building an emergency cash fund and/or investing for retirement and managing other expenses. The same benchmark applies to renting. So if your take-home (net) income is $4,500 a month, your total housing cost (mortgage/rent) should be no more than $1,620.

You only have so much money. If you overspend in any one area, it throws off your ability to have a balanced budget that includes saving and investing. Since housing is typically the largest part of people's budgets, it's vital that you don't overspend in this budget area. It's one of the reasons I believe in shared housing. In many areas, sticking to that 36 percent rule is nearly impossible for the average household.

Besides, a multigenerational household can strengthen your family finances and bonds. Many people struggle to make ends meet yet cling to living in a single-family household situation, even if it means financial devastation.

Young adults shouldn't be viewed as irresponsible or financial failures for living with their parents well into their twenties or even thirties. In fact, if everyone is content with the arrangement and there's room and respect, why move out? If young adults are otherwise responsible, why should they flail about financially trying to keep up with crushing rent and/or student loan payments?

Also, seniors who can no longer safely live alone should be open to moving in with their adult children and/or grandchildren. The arrangement can be a benefit for everyone in the household.

"Multigenerational living arrangements might improve financial resources, buffer stress, reduce loneliness, enhance intellectual sharing, and generate structural social capital, thereby elevating the level of one's health," according to findings in the journal *SSM – Population Health.*

Shared living arrangements enable people to better share the cost of housing, food, and transportation and the responsibilities for child and elder care. When a crisis hits, those who manage to hold on to their jobs can help the household weather the storm.

The goal is not to be house-poor, meaning that so much of your net pay is devoted to your housing costs that you can't save.

The Gig Economy

Thirty-six percent of U.S. workers participate in the so-called gig economy. That includes everyone from online platform workers — selling items on eBay or Etsy — to drivers for Uber or Lyft, to contract nurses, to those who take a temp job, according to a 2018 Gallup poll. It's basically all people who work outside a traditional full-time or part-time job.

Gallup says its data shows "a tale of two gig economies." There are independent gig workers and then there are temporary or contingent workers. Independent gig workers, being their own boss, enjoy more flexibility and freedom, Gallup notes. Contingent gig workers work like traditional employees, but they don't enjoy the same benefits, pay, and job security. "Supporters claim the gig economy is a trend toward worker empowerment and entrepreneurship, while critics worry it signals the deterioration of the social contract between employees and employers," says Gallup.

Most people (53 percent) report that the money they earn in the gig economy is a secondary source of income, according to a 2018 Marketplace-Edison Research poll. But among workers 18 to 34 years old, 53 percent said their work in the gig economy is their primary source of income. Here are some other findings from that poll:

- Gig workers are more likely to be stressed about job security, saving, and managing their expenses than people with traditional employment. If the gig job is their primary source of income, people reported an even higher stress level.
- Eighty percent of gig employees whose gig work is their primary source of income say that an unexpected expense of $1,000 would be difficult to pay.
- Eighty-five percent of gig employees whose gig work is their primary source of income say they worry about how an economic recession in the U.S. would affect them.
- Fifty-one percent of gig workers say they work harder for their income than those in traditional jobs.

These results aren't surprising, because with flexibility often comes income instability.

This section addresses issues faced by workers who by either choice or necessity find themselves working in the gig economy.

I'm worried that I may be laid off. How much can I earn working a side gig?

Increasingly, even workers with full-time salaried jobs are relying on side hustles, according to a report (*The Gig Economy and the Future of Retirement*) by the online financial management firm Betterment. Nearly one in four Americans earns money from the digital platform economy, according to the Pew Research Center. You might be driving for Uber or Lyft. You rent your home or apartment through Airbnb. Or you deliver food for DoorDash. You may be a freelance writer or contract employee. Perhaps you've built up a business walking dogs or taking care of other people's pooches while they are on vacation. You might deliver groceries through Instacart or Postmates. If service is your gift, you can work for TaskRabbit, a gig platform that connects consumers with people who can do odd jobs or run errands. New Yorkers even hired TaskRabbit workers to stand in COVID-19 testing lines for them.

Where once a side hustle was what someone did while in between steady nine-to-five jobs, many people have now decided that the gig economy is the way they want to work. Or because of a job loss, it's the only work they can get. But the hard reality is, whether out of desire or necessity, it's important to figure out if you can live well enough on income earned in the gig economy.

The San Francisco–based loan provider Earnest looked at the earnings of gig workers based on tens of thousands of loan applicants. The big takeaway from the survey: 85 percent of side-gig workers make less than $500 per month. The standout was Airbnb hosts, who make on average $924 each month. TaskRabbit workers came in second, earning $380 per month. Lyft and Uber drivers make an average of $377 and $364, respectively. As you can see from these numbers, it will take a lot of hustle to earn enough to cover your monthly expenses.

These jobs can make a difference for your financial picture. Just don't overestimate how much you can earn in the gig economy.

I'll leave you with this from a Pew report: "Proponents of these digital earning platforms argue that they offer important benefits, such as the freedom and flexibility to work at a time and place of one's choosing or the ability to turn a hobby or pastime into a source of income. But others worry that this emerging 'gig economy' represents a troubling shift in which workers face increased financial instability and are required to shoulder more of the burden for ensuring their own pay and benefits."

Should I quit my full-time job to work my side gigs?

Many adults work in the gig economy to supplement their income, according to the Federal Reserve. Younger adults are more likely to have side gigs, with 37 percent of 18- to 29-year-olds performing gig work, compared to 21 percent of people 60 or older.

Even with the irregular income, it may be tempting to give up a traditional job for the flexibility of a side hustle. You become the master of your time. You work when you want to work. You take the jobs you like, or, realistically, the ones that pay the bills.

But it's important to note that workers in the gig economy often don't have benefits such as health insurance, sick leave, overtime, workers' compensation, or access to a workplace retirement plan with perhaps a matching contribution from an employer. On this latter point, you can certainly still save for retirement even if you don't have a 401(k) or similar employer-sponsored retirement plan. However, surveys show that people save more when encouraged by an employer.

If you want to work this way, just consider what you may be giving up by not working in a traditional job with benefits.

Consider the pros and cons of giving up your full-time job for gig work

PROS:
- Flexibility. You work when you want to work.
- There's little or no managerial oversight for many jobs.
- You can do multiple things – drive for Uber one day, do temporary work in an office another day.

CONS:
- You aren't guaranteed work.
- You have to budget well to manage your irregular income.
- There are no employer-provided benefits, such as health insurance or a retirement savings plan.
- You don't have paid sick leave.
- You're responsible for paying estimated taxes rather than having an employer withhold taxes for you.

Gig work can be fulfilling, but you must be a hustler to make it work. You know this already, but I have to say it. Hustling is a key part of being a self-employed or gig worker. Even if you have a good gig or contract, you need to be constantly looking for the next one. You are selling yourself, and you'd better be good at it.

How do I manage my budget when my income fluctuates?
If your income fluctuates, you need to become very disciplined with budgeting. The principles of money management aren't vastly different; you just need to devise a system for handling your irregular income.

This is the budgeting system I recommend:

- **Set a baseline for expenses.** The key to managing money when your income goes up and down is establishing a baseline of how much money it takes to run your household. Ask yourself, at a minimum level, how much you need to pay for the essential and important things every month — rent/mortgage, transportation, utilities, food, insurance, cable, etc. You can build in some frills, but you must be prepared to cut them out if you don't earn enough to cover all your necessary expenses in a month. For instance, you can include eating out or entertainment, but realize that there will be months when your earnings are going to be lower and you'll have to eliminate those nonessential expenses to balance your budget. Total up the monthly expenses and you'll have a good idea about how much you need to earn at a minimum.

  If you have expenses that are not due every month, such as an annual or semiannual insurance payment, just divide the yearly amount by twelve and include it in your budget. For example, if your car insurance is $1,200 a year and you pay it annually, your monthly budget should include $100 to be saved exclusively for this expense. Do this for any bill that you don't pay every month but that you know will be due in a lump sum later in the year.

- **Budget from a main household account.** Establish a checking account from which you pay all your monthly expenses.

- **Create a "sweep account."** Deposit all your earnings from your side gig into one account. It is from this account that you will sweep out to the main household account the amount you need for your monthly budget.

Let's say your gig income for one month is $3,000 after taxes. Your baseline monthly budget expenses are $2,000. Once you get paid, you should transfer the $2,000 you need into the main household account. If you kept the extra $1,000 in your household account, you might be tempted to spend it, because it feels like a bonus. But let's say the following month you earn only $1,000. You now have the extra $1,000 that's sitting in the sweep account to make up the difference you need for that month. The point is that in the months when your income is more than you need for your baseline expenses, you must be disciplined enough not to spend the extra money you don't need now and will need later.

Once your income hits the sweep account, divide it up and transfer it where it's needed, including to the emergency fund and the "life happens" fund that I hope you're building, both of which I've discussed earlier.

- **Don't splurge on your good months.** It's so tempting during the higher earning periods to go hog wild doing things you couldn't do when money wasn't coming in at the same level. This is probably the single biggest mistake people with side gigs make. Actually, it's also the biggest mistake many people with nine-to-five jobs make. But what they have that gig workers don't have is a regular paycheck. They can catch up on an overspending episode because they have a guaranteed paycheck coming in. Gig workers do not.

- **Set up a tax account.** Finally, you absolutely need to make sure you are subtracting and saving the money for income taxes (federal and state). Do it as soon as you are paid if taxes aren't withheld. So many people have come to me distraught because they have been hit with a huge tax bill and penalties. You probably know people who don't report all their gig income. But do you want to be the one the IRS catches? The IRS is tough on tax evaders when they are caught.

Be smart: Before you spend a penny of your income, set aside the taxes you need to pay. Transfer the estimated taxes you'll be responsible for to a bank account set up specifically and only for tax payments. Do not touch this money.

Now, I know it will be tempting to use this money when you have lower-income months. Realistically, if you can't pay rent or need food, you probably will tap it. However, as soon as you can, *replace the funds*.

So far I've suggested that you have at least three separate checking accounts: main household, sweep, and one for taxes. You should also have separate rainy-day accounts. That's a lot of pots, so shop for a bank or credit union that doesn't charge monthly maintenance fees for multiple accounts. With online banking there should not be an issue with transferring funds among the accounts.

Do I really have to pay taxes on my side gig?

Here's what the Internal Revenue Service says about taxes you owe: "You must pay tax on income you earn from gig work. If you do gig work as an employee, your employer should with-hold tax from your paycheck. If you do gig work as an inde-pendent contractor, you may have to pay estimated taxes." That's clear, right? Yes, you owe taxes on your gig income.

The IRS has created a very helpful portal for gig workers. Go to irs.gov and search for "Gig Economy Tax Center."

The IRS also has a third-party reporting system in which companies report income paid to people earning more than $600. This means that if you're a contractor, freelancer, or similar worker and you received more than $600 from a side job during the tax year, the individual or company that paid you generally must mail to you IRS Form 1099-NEC (which stands for nonemployee compensation). The 1099-NEC replaced the 1099-MISC for independent contractors starting in 2020. The 1099-MISC still exists but for other purposes.

The U.S. has a pay-as-you-go tax system, meaning that if you make enough to be taxed, you have to pay income tax due throughout the year as the money is earned. If you're a wage earner, your employer takes the responsibility for collecting the taxes out of your paycheck and sending them to the tax authorities. But if you earn money from gig work as an independent contractor, you may have to pay quarterly estimated taxes. You can avoid a penalty by paying enough tax on time. Just a note: The self-employed have to pay the employer and employee portions of FICA and Medicare taxes. The self-employment tax rate consists of two parts: 12.4 percent for Social Security (old age, survivors', and disability insurance) and 2.9 percent for Medicare (hospital insurance), the IRS points out.

Estimated tax payments are due four times a year. If due dates fall on a Saturday, Sunday, or legal holiday, the payments are due the next business day:

- April 15 for payment period January 1–March 31
- June 15 for payment period April 1–May 31

- September 15 for payment period June 1–August 31
- January 15 for payment period September 1–December 31

I can understand that this is all rather complicated. If you can't handle this yourself, hire a tax professional to make sure you get your taxes in on time.

On the website for the Center on Budget and Policy Priorities you'll find a help resource post. Go to cbpp.org and search for "Resources to Help Gig Workers Understand Taxes." The information is aimed at ridesharing gig workers, but it's helpful for anyone who is self-employed.

I'm in tax trouble. I didn't pay taxes for my side gig and now I owe the IRS. What can I do?

Getting a hefty tax bill from the IRS can be very scary. But don't panic. Okay, you're going to panic, but please know that you have options, and they all start with contacting the IRS.

The one thing you should not do is call a tax debt-relief company. Despite their promises, you are not likely to get away with paying pennies on the dollar. I understand why you might fall for the pitch. You want to believe that somebody can fix this problem quickly and make it go away. A tax debt-relief company will tell you that it has skilled agents or attorneys who can make a deal with the IRS so that you pay less than what you owe.

Forget it. Don't call. If you do, you'll end up paying hundreds, if not thousands, of dollars to the company for something you could have done yourself. Or, worse, the tax debt-relief company is a complete con and will take your money and do nothing.

Let me be clear. There are people who need to hire a tax

professional or company that specializes in representing tax-payers before the IRS for various tax issues. I'm recommending that you avoid companies that run the ads and have boiler-room operations that make promises they can't keep. Many are scams or, if legal, won't help you as much as they promise in the ads.

I've interviewed lots of people who tried debt-relief companies. It did not go well — at all! What typically happens is, you make the call to the tax relief company. You provide the firm with your tax documents. Then you wait and wait. You try calling — several times. If you reach someone, there's another false promise that they are processing your paperwork or that they are waiting for a response from the IRS.

They have your money and you still have the tax debt. Or maybe they help you set up a payment plan, but you could have done that yourself. You could have taken the money you paid to the debt-relief company and reduced your tax debt with the IRS.

If you've received a balance-due notice in the mail from the IRS, you will find a toll-free number to call. Please, call. Fight your fear. You'll probably have to wait on hold for a long time. Wait. One woman I helped owed the IRS about $25,000. Of course she didn't have the money. Even as tears were running down her face, I made her call the IRS. Within about 15 minutes she had set up a payment plan. She also set up a payment plan for the state taxes she owed. Then I told her not to renew her apartment lease but to move in with her sister and aggressively pay off the tax debt. Not long after she began her payment plans, she applied for a federal job. When the agency pulled her credit report, the tax debt was listed. She ultimately got the job. If she had not had a payment plan in place, she would not have been hired.

The IRS can be intimidating, but the truth is, the agency has a lot of ways for you to catch up on your tax debt. It offers various options for those who can't pay what they owe. You can set up an online payment agreement for up to 72 months if you owe $50,000 or less in combined taxes, penalties, and interest. Go to irs.gov and search for "Online Payment Agreement Application." You can also request a payment agreement by filling out IRS Form 9465, which you can find online at irs.gov.

You also can ask the IRS for an "offer in compromise," or OIC. This allows the agency to accept less than your full tax obligation under certain circumstances. The OIC is what the debt relief companies mean when they say they can help you settle your tax debt for less. But what they don't tell you is that you can apply for this yourself. Besides, most people don't end up getting an OIC, because the IRS determines that they can pay their debt over time. Although the OIC is a legitimate program offered by the IRS, it's intended solely to help folks who are so financially down that it's unlikely the agency could collect all that the government is owed.

If you're facing great economic hardship, you may qualify for an OIC. You must provide detailed financial information to prove your economic situation, and you must exhaust all other payment options. The IRS will look at your income, expenses, ability to pay, and, most importantly, whether you have any assets — including equity in your home — in order to determine whether you qualify. You can use the IRS's OIC pre-qualifier tool on its website to find out whether you're eligible.

If a financial crisis has truly made it difficult for you to pay your rent or to put food on the table, you can request that your delinquent account be placed in "Currently Not Collectible" status. The IRS will temporarily delay collection until your financial condition improves. However, interest and penalties are still accruing. For more information about this option, go to irs.gov and search for "Temporarily Delay the Collection Process." To request a delay or to discuss payment options, call the IRS at 1-800-829-1040.

For more information on this action, contact the Taxpayer Advocate Service, which is an independent organization within the IRS that works directly with the agency to help taxpayers resolve various issues. Go to taxpayeradvocate.irs.gov and search for "Currently Not Collectible" for more information about the process.

My friend invited me to a presentation. I think it's a multilevel marketing opportunity. Should I go?

The Federal Trade Commission, the Securities and Exchange Commission, and the Better Business Bureau have issued warnings about multilevel marketing schemes. However, it is difficult to distinguish legitimate multilevel marketing schemes from pyramid schemes, which is why you need to be very cautious.

Under a multilevel marketing enterprise, would-be entrepreneurs pay to become a sales representative or member of the company with the right to sell a certain product and recruit others to do the same. But the sales side of the business is often secondary to the recruitment of new participants. Those at the top of the pyramid can make substantial money, but mostly on the backs of people at the bottom, who are recruited primarily to entice others into the business.

As attractive as multilevel marketing sounds, with its network of team members, you should know that most people really don't make a lot of money. Among the more than 20 million Americans who participate or have participated in multilevel marketing organizations, 90 percent say they got involved to make money, according to a study released by the AARP Foundation. Here's the problem: Nearly half (47 percent) lost money, and a quarter (27 percent) made no money at all, the AARP found. Of those who did make money, more than half (53 percent) made less than $5,000.

If you think that pursuing this type of gig is going to work for you, then okay, try it. Just know that for most people it does not deliver substantial income.

See the section in this book on scams for more information about protecting yourself from shady business opportunities.

How can I save for retirement as a gig worker when I'm barely making any money?

According to a report by Betterment, almost 40 percent of gig workers feel unprepared to save enough to maintain their lifestyle during retirement.

When you are in a crisis, you can't beat yourself up for not having the money to do all the essential things that personal finance columnists or experts say you must do to have a secure retirement. Of course saving and investing for retirement is important. But I don't want you to worry yourself sick when times are so tough that you can barely make your rent. The present is more important. Once the crisis passes, or once you can start to at least see that you'll have more than you need to make ends meet, you can reassess your retirement savings situation.

At this point, start looking at what retirement income you can expect. That starts with Social Security. This may not make you feel better, but at least you won't feel alone when I tell you that in 2020, according to Gallup, nearly six in ten retirees relied on Social Security as their major income source.

Research funded by the Center for Retirement Research at Boston College found that in 2014, independent contractors underreported their income and as a result didn't pay $3.9 billion in Social Security taxes. Tax compliance is a pain. It's bothersome and confusing. And I understand, you need all the money you earn, especially when gig work doesn't pay as well as a wage job probably would. So it's tempting to skip paying taxes. But please think long-term. Pay into the Social Security system. If you don't, you could cost yourself significant retirement earnings later. If you haven't been able to save and invest adequately for retirement, those monthly Social Security checks can make a huge difference. In fact, a lack of retirement savings is the reason a third of side hustlers have a second job, according to Betterment's 2018 *The Gig Economy and The Future of Retirement*. Social Security uses your earnings and work history to determine your eligibility for retirement or disability benefits or your family's eligibility for survivor benefits when you die. In 2021, workers received one credit for each $1,470 of earnings each year, up to the maximum of four credits per year, according to the Social Security Administration. Each year the amount of earnings needed for credits goes up slightly as average earnings levels increase. If you are self-employed, you earn Social Security credits the same way employees do (one credit for each $1,470 in net earnings, but no more than four credits per year).

Now that you know you can collect Social Security benefits if you pay into the system, you should get your annual Social Security statement, which shows your estimated benefit amount, how much you'll get if you became disabled, and vital information about spousal and survivor benefits. Although you won't find out the exact final amounts until you apply for benefits, the estimates on your statement will help you plan for retirement.

Congress has gone back and forth about mailing Social Security statements. You should go online and open a Social Security account. To get your statement electronically, go to ssa.gov and you'll find a link to create an account on the home page.

If you've placed a freeze or fraud alert on your credit file, you will not be able to open the account until you unlock the file. Social Security uses information in your credit report to verify your identity. You can open an account in person by going to a local Social Security office.

As a self-employed person, you can still save for retirement in a tax-advantaged plan. You can fund a SEP IRA, which allows you to contribute up to 25 percent of your net self-employment income, to a maximum annual contribution of $58,000 in 2021. There's also the option of a solo 401(k), which allows you to contribute 100 percent of earned income. A solo 401(k) has the same rules and requirements as any other 401(k) plan. There's more paperwork with a solo 401(k), so get some help from a tax professional to set it up.

The Benefits of Selling Online

When money is tight, one way to look for some cash is to sell your stuff. Think about it. You have a lot of things — in the closets, under the bed, or in your garage. You might even have stuff piled high in an offsite self-storage facility (although if you do and you don't often need those items, clean it out and stop paying for your belongings to have their own place — with air conditioning).

Fortunately, lots of shoppers are very comfortable buying things secondhand from online platforms. The coronavirus pandemic forced many people to change their shopping habits, with millions more shoppers going online to make purchases.

The secondhand market is estimated to hit a whopping $64 billion by 2024, according to the 2020 Resale Report by the secondhand clothing marketplace thredUP. That's a significant jump from $28 billion in 2019. "For all the challenges Covid posed to our assumptions about consumer behavior, one thing is clear: consumers everywhere are prioritizing value and accelerating the shift to thrift. When times get uncertain, we all focus on our family balance sheet," said Anthony S. Marino, thredUP's president.

According to a 2020 survey by the commerce platform

Poshmark, 75 percent of shoppers are comfortable purchasing items directly from people online. The survey also found that 58 percent of consumers are comfortable purchasing items through social media platforms.

This is good news, whether you want to sell a few items in a hurry or want to become a regular online seller as a side gig. There are more opportunities than ever before for you to supplement your income or earn some needed cash.

Following is some guidance to get you started.

Where can I sell things online?

The marketplace for selling items online has been dominated by several well-known players — Amazon, eBay, Craigslist, and Etsy. There's also Instagram and Facebook Marketplace. Poshmark has become a leading platform for sellers and shoppers of women's, men's, and children's clothing. There are also The RealReal and Plato's Closet, where you can get paid for gently used clothing, and the digital resale platform thredUP. Got electronics to sell? Try selling the items on Decluttr or Nextworth.

As you decide which site to use to sell items, pay attention to the fees, which vary. Factor in all the costs, which of course will affect how much money you'll net. Time is money too. If you're spending a lot of time running around mailing items or meeting up with people, you might not be making as much as you think.

Bear in mind that ecommerce platforms are ever-evolving and new players are constantly entering the space. So again, as I always recommend, please do some research. Find out what's the latest popular place to sell your items. Then spend some time getting to understand the ins and outs of the platform. How do you post your items? What's the best way to ship things to people? If you're only selling locally, what's the best way to safely meet up with a buyer and be paid?

You might just have some things around the house that you want to sell to generate some quick cash, or you might decide to become a regular online seller. If you think you'll be a regular seller, be sure you conduct business in a professional way in order to get the best reviews. People read reviews! If you say you'll ship items in a certain timeframe, be sure to honor that promise as best you can.

Is it safe to sell online?

Think of online selling as being the Wild, Wild West. It can be rough out there. So be very careful. There are a lot of people who are legitimately looking for items to buy, but scammers are also lurking, waiting to take advantage of unsuspecting and trusting people. The con artists are very good at their jobs, so do your homework.

Take precautions so that you're not scammed. The Better Business Bureau offers the following advice:

Don't take money orders or checks. It's too hard for the average person to know whether a check or money order is legit. Use a third-party payment application such as PayPal, Apple Pay, or Google Pay to sell your items. Peer-to-peer payments through apps such as Venmo and Square Cash App make it easier and safer to send and accept money. Many banking institutions use Zelle, another digital payment network.

Never, ever accept an overpayment. In this kind of scam, a buyer sends a check for more than an item is worth. Then, feigning an error, the scammer asks you to send back the over-age. This is always a scam. Always. See the question below to see how the scam works.

Don't communicate with a prospective buyer outside of the official selling platform. To protect their users, many online selling platforms require users to communicate via the platform's own messaging system. It's a good idea. "When you communicate and accept payments outside of the platform, you are at greater risk for fraud and forfeit protections that the platform can provide," the Better Business Bureau says.

Meet in a safe public place. Find out if your local police department has set up a "safe exchange or zone" program, where you can meet a buyer in the parking lot or the lobby of the police station. Hundreds of police departments have what they call SafeTrade Stations. The website safetradestations.com compiles a list of police stations nationwide that allow people to meet for such exchanges, although it is not a complete list. Click on the link "Where to Trade."

Your local department may call its safe zone by another name. For example, one police department in Maryland maintains what it calls a Transaction Safe Place.

What specific scams should I look out for?

Although new scams pop up routinely, there are some tried-and-true ones that continue to ensnare people. In one scam, a potential buyer tries to persuade the seller to use his or her shipping company, claiming it's cheaper. But the buyer reroutes the package and then files a complaint with the ecommerce platform saying that the item was never received.

One of the most ubiquitous scams is the overpayment scheme. You post something to sell. You get a bite from a buyer. The person sends you a check or money order for the item, but it's for more than the agreed-upon price. No problem, the buyer says. It's his mistake. Keep what's yours and send the overpayment back. So you deposit the check, the bank seems to clear it, and you're feeling good — until your bank contacts you to say that the buyer's check was a fraud. You've been scammed.

"You might think that you're in the clear once a check's funds have deposited into your account, but it often takes longer for a bank to realize that a check is bad," the Better Business Bureau says in a consumer alert. "This lag in time between when a check reaches your account and when it's discovered to be a forgery is exactly what scammers are counting on."

Just because you withdraw the funds deposited via a check does not mean the check is good. Federal regulations require financial institutions to make funds from a deposit available generally within one to five business days. However, it can take weeks before a bank discovers that a deposited check is worthless.

The Federal Trade Commission said that people reported more than 27,000 fake check scams in 2019, with reported losses topping $28 million. The agency said that 18 percent of the complaints involved people who said they got a fake check as payment for something they were selling online. On an individual level, the median losses were nearly $2,000. And who is most likely to be a victim? The FTC says that consumers in their twenties are more than twice as likely as people 30 and older to report losing money to fake check scams. Scammers contact young adults directly through their college or university email accounts, with messages made to look like official school communications.

You might be wondering, "Isn't it the bank's job to verify

checks?" A check is only provisionally cleared at first, and you could be scammed if it's later found to be fraudulent. If you fall victim to this scam, see if the bank will allow you to make good on the bad check with a payment installment plan.

What should I do if I've been scammed?

You are probably embarrassed, kicking yourself for falling for the scam and being duped. But don't beat yourself up. The scammers are very good at what they do. Running their schemes is their full-time job.

If you are scammed, please report it. The authorities may not be able to help you, but your complaint along with others may stop the scammers from victimizing other people.

The Federal Trade Commission is the main government agency that collects scam reports. Report your scam online at ReportFraud.ftc.gov or by phone at 1-877-382-4357. Also contact your state consumer protection office. If you've lost money or other possessions in a scam, report it to your local police too. You can also report the scam to BBB.org/scamtracker.

Is the money I make selling my stuff taxable?

Generally, if you're selling used items for less than what you paid for them, you don't owe taxes on the sales, according to the online tax site 1040.com. However, if you are going into business to sell items online, you'll owe income taxes on what you make. You may also need to pay sales tax. In this case, please talk to a tax professional. The last thing you want to have is an unexpected letter from the IRS demanding past-due taxes with penalties.

You can find some helpful tax tips about selling online at 1040.com. TurboTax also posts a fact sheet at turbotax.intuit. com for people selling on eBay. The guidance may apply to other online platforms.

What can I sell to make money?

Sure, the dresser in the bedroom you never use could fetch enough money to pay a bill, but you might be able to sell other items in your home to raise some cash. Here are some ideas.

Clothes and jewelry. What's old to you could be vintage to someone else. Also think about the era of the items you have in your closet. Perhaps around October, when people are looking for Halloween costumes, you can get rid of that neon-purple disco shirt that you've been hanging on to, or the bell-bottom pants.

Gift cards. There is an aftermarket for gift cards people have but don't want or can't use. Some sites that buy unwanted gift cards are Raise.com, GiftCard Granny, and Cardpool.

Parking space. If you live near a metropolitan area where a lot of commuters are looking for parking, maybe you can sell your space while you're at work. If you have a parking space but no car, you can rent your space. Just be sure it's allowed under any community covenant or rental property agreement.

Books, including old textbooks. If you haven't already, check around the house to see if you have any books you can sell. With the cost of textbooks so high, struggling college students are always looking for a deal. Even an older edition might help someone.

Old records. Vinyl records are making a comeback. "In 2019, 18.8 million LPs were sold in the United States, up 14 percent compared to 2018 and more than 20-fold compared to 2006 when the vinyl comeback began," according to a Statista report.

CDs, DVDs, and games. Your old music, movies, and games could be someone else's treasure.

Are consignment shops a good way to sell stuff and make money?

Most people are familiar with shopping in traditional second-hand shops, that is, buying items that other people have donated. But you can also sell your possessions in brick-and-mortar stores and make money.

You'll have to do some legwork. Start by searching online for "consignment stores near me." Then start making some calls. I suggest you drive by and check out the shop before taking your items there to sell. Get recommendations from people who have sold items there.

You may want to try to sell certain items at a consignment store that specializes in those items. For example, sell your vintage vinyl albums in a used music store.

Typically you get paid in one of two ways, either up front or by sharing in the money the shop receives for the item when it's sold.

If you're not up for the ecommerce marketplace, consignment selling is a good way to declutter while making some money.

The Schemes and Scams

You need money—like, yesterday. You've lost your job. Or
the gig jobs you've pieced together don't cover all your expenses. You may still be working but living from paycheck to
paycheck. So offers for easy money seem like just the financial lifeline you need. Or maybe a work-at-home opportunity
promises that you can earn enough to pay the bills. It's a business opportunity that will make you your own boss; all you
have to do is recruit others who also yearn to build wealth
through entrepreneurship.

Annually scams affect one in four households, according
to a study by the Better Business Bureau's Institute for Marketplace Trust. Unfortunately, most consumers believe they
are invincible—that they would never be duped or become
the victim of a scam. "Individuals tend to believe that others are more at risk of being scammed than themselves," the
BBB report said. "They also view scam victims through a dis-
torted lens—as elderly, alone, and pitiable, or gullible, unin-
telligent, and worthy of scorn." The fact is we are *all* at risk,
the BBB says, and "those most likely to be victimized tend to
be younger and better educated."

According to a Federal Trade Commission report, younger

people (20 to 29 years old) reported losing money to fraud more often than people 70 to 79 – 33 percent compared to 13 percent. The FTC found in a 2020 report that the number of complaints about scams that started on social media has skyrocketed. Consumers reported losing more than $117 million to this type of scam in just the first six months of 2020, compared to $134 million for all of 2019, the agency said.

An economic crisis is a gold mine for con artists. During the coronavirus pandemic, consumers increasingly reported social media messages that offered grant money and other giveaways. "As people seek more ways to earn money, reports about multilevel marketing companies and pyramid schemes – including blessing circles and other gifting schemes – on social media have increased," the FTC said. "The numbers were up a staggering fivefold in the second quarter of 2020. Many of these recruitment offers reportedly came with extravagant claims about likely earnings, which is always a red flag."

If you are the victim of a scam, immediately report it to the FTC, which has created a fraud reporting platform for consumers at ReportFraud.ftc.gov. If you file a complaint, you'll receive advice about what to do next based on the kind of fraud you report.

The Better Business Bureau offers advice that you should take to heart. To avoid losing money in your effort to increase your earnings, you must be receptive to vital information about scams and schemes. In short, you must recognize your own vulnerability. No matter how badly you need cash, you can make a bad situation a lot worse by falling for schemes or scams that make money only for the promoters.

Are there any legitimate work-at-home jobs?

Legitimate home-based job opportunities do exist. You can work in a virtual call center. If you have good writing skills, you can be a freelance writer or editor. Some data-entry jobs can be done from home. The spread of COVID-19 resulted in a lot of companies sending staff home to work remotely. Many of the workers may not return to the office, and new hires may find they can work from home too. Thirty percent of executives foresee the need for less office space owing to remote work. This opens the door for people with a need or desire to work from home.

But please approach any home-based job or business opportunities with a great amount of skepticism. Many, if not most, of the promotions you see for ways to make money from home are either schemes (not illegal but highly suspect, and make money only for the promoters) or scams (their only purpose is to take your money).

Law enforcement officials repeat one warning that can apply to most work-from-home offers: "If it seems too good to be true, it probably is." The problem with this statement is that desperate people want to believe that the business or job opportunities are legitimate. When you've lost your job or your income has dropped during an economic crisis, sometimes all you have to cling to is hope.

What may appear to be too good to be true for people who are not struggling becomes believable for folks who are. It's not gullibility but desperation that makes people believe that they can make thousands of dollars a month stuffing envelopes or doing medical billing for a physician. That multilevel marketing business will make them rich, they hope.

I'm going to give you some tips on how to spot a fake work-at-home business, but here's what I need you to do. Before you respond to a business or job offer, reach out to the most skeptical person you know. I'm talking about someone who if you said the sky is blue would go to the window and double-check. Got that person in mind? Good. Now tell this person about the home-based business. If you're going to a business start-up meeting or plan to sign up for a Zoom conference call, invite your skeptical friend along.

This one suggestion alone can save you a lot of money and heartache. I should know, because I am the designated skeptic in my family and among my friends. I believe nothing until it's proven true by independent research. My training as a journalist helps me spot a scam. But I am also a natural-born doubter. Skepticism is in my soul.

I've gone to such business opportunity meetings. I've listened in on the calls. I've reviewed the promotional materials. As a result, I've saved friends and family from being scammed or talked into signing up for a business venture that would have sucked them dry of their savings. In fact I won a major journalism award for a series of columns that resulted from attending a home-based business meeting that turned out to be illegal.

Here's what happened. A friend was having a recruiting session at her home. She was concerned that it wasn't legit and asked me to come and listen to the pitch. "If I can show you how to make a 400 percent return on your money in seven days, would you be interested?" the promoter asked the group at the start of the meeting. She said there wasn't any risk in what she was promoting. "I guarantee you'll make money," she promised.

Stop. Right away I knew that this wasn't going to be good.

One of the first things a wise investor knows is that if some-one says you can make a high return with little to no risk, it's always — and I mean *always* — risky and probably a scam or a shady scheme. High return equals high risk.

Nonetheless, the people who were crowded in the living room perked up, eager to hear how they could make so much money — in just seven days! To earn that unbelievable return, they would have to pay a $100 fee up front to become a "mem-ber" of the enterprise. Then they had to recruit five people to join too, and then two of those five would have to refinance their mortgages through the company the woman was rep-resenting. This would earn the members a $500 bonus. Thus their $100 investment would net them $400 ($500 minus their initial $100 entry free), or a 400 percent return.

People were promised that, like the promoter, they could end up earning big bucks by also giving wealth-building pre-sentations. "Every time I go to see people, I make money," the promoter said.

The problem was that the whole thing involved a network of unlicensed, improperly trained mortgage brokers. After I exposed the scheme, several former salespeople who were try-ing to make extra money from a home-based business said they were disappointed at their own blindness — and in some cases at their own greed. It was a completely illegal opera-tion. As a result of my investigation, the operation was shut down in Maryland, and a bank account executive was fired. The head of the operation moved on to other states and was again sanctioned. But he kept recruiting people who wanted to believe that they could earn a lot of money quickly and with little effort.

I share this story with you so that you put on a cloak of cynicism. I understand that you are worried about paying your bills. But you must approach any work-at-home business opportunity with a great deal of suspicion. Assume it's a scam and then work from there.

Certain signs indicate that a work-at-home offer may be a scam, according to the FTC.

- You are chastised for or discouraged from asking too many questions during the meeting. Go no further if you're shut down while trying to get your questions answered.
- You are promised large earnings.
- You received an unsolicited email. Just don't do it. Don't click on the links.
- You are required to pay an up-front fee or entry fee, which is likely to enrich the company, not you.
- You must give the promoter your credit card to help pay for the costs of starting up the business, such as buying supplies.
- You are pressured into signing up for pricey services or training. If the informational session mostly involves having you sign up for additional training sessions, get out.

If you're considering a work-at-home offer, go to consumer .ftc.gov/features/feature-0019-business-opportunity-scams. Read through the article and click on the link for FTC's "Business Opportunity Rule," which requires promoters to give you a one-page disclosure document with information regarding any legal action against the company, its cancellation or refund policy, and whether the company has made any promises about what you'll earn. If you are going to a business opportunity session in person, print out the disclosure statement and use it to get in writing what you're being told. Go to ftc.gov and search for an article entitled "Work-at-Home Businesses." On the page, scroll down to the link for "How to Know If It's a Scam," where you will find the link for the one-page disclosure document.

For more information about business opportunities in general, call 1-877-FTC-HELP (877-382-4357). You should also contact your state's attorney general to see whether there have been any complaints about a particular business opportunity. To find your AG's office, go to the National Association of Attorneys General website, naag.org. At the top of the home page you will see a link for "Find My AG."

Okay, now that I've gotten you sufficiently paranoid, here's where you can find information on home-based opportunities that *might* work. However, please double-check the citations, because information can change quickly.

- Clark Howard's website, clark.com. Search for "Work From Home Guide," a list of legitimate work-at-home jobs. Howard has a popular consumer radio show and he has assembled a team to help in his Consumer Action Center. The article will direct you to companies offering home-based jobs, many in the customer service field.
- FlexJobs.com. This is a subscription-based job opportunity site. The site reviews the job postings to weed out scams. Its focus is on helping people find jobs with flexible working options. You may balk at paying a monthly or yearly fee, but it's worth it if it weeds out the scams. The pricing can change, and the site may have

sales. FlexJobs.com offers a one-week subscription for $6.95. During one sale, the monthly fee was $14.95 and annual membership was going for $49.95.

- Try job-search sites such as Monster, CareerBuilder, Indeed, and Glassdoor. Look for jobs for which you can telecommute, meaning work from home.
- Look for articles about work-from-home opportunities in well-respected blogs (such as thepennyhoarder.com) or major newspapers or network sites.

Be safe out there. I know it's a pain to keep hearing that you need to do some research. You're tired. You're frustrated. You're scared. Yet that's exactly when you are more likely to be victimized.

Okay, but what about multilevel marketing opportunities? Are they legitimate?

I am not a fan of these kinds of business models. I am biased against them because of my experience working with dozens of people who bought into the dream that turned into a nightmare of recruiting and purchasing products themselves to keep up their sales figures.

I have been to a lot of meetings about these business opportunities. A friend did well in one multilevel marketing program, even earning herself the use of a leased car for a year. But even my friend, although successful at first, eventually got tired of the relentless pace to recruit new people and sell products. She was doing this while holding on to her full-time job. She had thought about quitting that job and making the side gig her main source of income. But the irregular income was too risky for her.

The Federal Trade Commission, the Securities and Exchange Commission, and the Better Business Bureau have issued many warnings over the years about multilevel marketing business opportunities. With a legitimate multilevel marketing business or direct-to-consumer sales company, participants make money selling products or services and by getting commissions on sales made by the people they recruit, often referred to as their "downlines." The problem is, it's very difficult to distinguish legitimate multilevel marketing businesses from pyramid schemes, which is why you need to be very cautious about joining, the FTC says.

One of the clearest indicators of a pyramid scheme is the expectation of a significant payout based on the recruitment of other people, who then must also bring in recruits. Eventually the pyramid collapses, because operators can't recruit enough people. Even worse, during a financial crisis, illegal pyramid schemes tend to increase, as they did during the coronavirus pandemic.

One important element to keep in mind is that a multilevel marketing business often relies on the trust and friendship that exist in groups of people who have something in common — family or social groups, religious groups, and the like. This is a type of "affinity fraud" and is often listed by the North American Securities Administrators Association as among the top 10 frauds. In a 2018 report entitled "Multilevel Marketing: The Research, Risks and Rewards," the AARP Foundation found that 73 percent of people involved in such a business opportunity either didn't make money or lost money.

If you like sales and enjoy talking to a lot of people, you can probably make a living in a multilevel marketing enterprise. Just know that most people don't make nearly as much money as they are promised in the promotional materials.

A friend suggested I join a sou-sou or blessing loom to make some money. Is this a legitimate way to build wealth?

Here's the cultural backstory of the sou-sou, also known as "Susu," "blessing loom," or "gifting circle." Promoters pitch the sou-sou as a common practice among Caribbean and African immigrants to help their businesses grow. It's also a common practice in certain other immigrant groups. The idea is that people pool their money together in an informal savings club. People are recruited and then encouraged to bring in others, with assurances that they can all make three-digit returns in a matter of weeks. During hard economic times, when lenders may pull back on lending, this version of the chain-letter pyramid scheme pops up. During the pandemic, illegal sou-sou pyramid schemes raged in the Black community, which was hard hit by COVID-related job losses.

The problem is, the promised large payout is simply redirected money collected from new recruits. There's no wealth-building, only the shifting of money from the newest recruits to people who got into the scheme early. Eventually the pyramid collapses, when not enough people can be persuaded to join.

A legitimate sou-sou occurs when members aspire to help each other save for a specific purpose and nobody receives more money than he or she put in. This informal savings model is often used in communities where people can't easily get loans to fund a business or don't have access to traditional banks.

In typical recruitment materials I've reviewed, 15 people are divided into four levels: one person is at the top level or center, two are on a second level, four are on the third, and eight are at the bottom. In one version, the incoming eight

recruits each had to send $500 – $4,000 total for the group
– to the person at the top. The money would be transferred
through PayPal, Venmo, or some other cash app. Eventually
the people at the bottom level were supposed to reach the top
of their own subgroup and receive their $4,000 payout.

The gifting circle or sou-sou can appear to be foolproof because early participants share testimonies of their substantial
gains. Promoters even hold weekly conference calls to rally
people with motivational presentations about how their in-
volvement will help build wealth in their community.

This Is a Real Sou-Sou/Gifting Circle/Blessing Loom

- The sou-sou is small, and the members personally and
  directly know each other. It does not include a friend of a
  friend or a cousin you haven't seen since the 1995 family
  reunion.
- You get back the same amount of money you put in.
  It's an informal savings club in which people take turns
  getting the pot of money.
- Traditional sou-sous are not meant to turn a profit for
  their members.

This Is a Fraudulent Sou-Sou/Pyramid Scheme

- You are promised a "gift" far exceeding what you put up.
  For example, you put in $500 and get back $4,000.
- You can't possibly know everyone who has joined.
- Recruiting is a necessary part of the so-called sou-sou.
  You need to bring in two people, and those two people
  need to bring in two more people, and those two people
  need to bring in two people, and then those two people

need to bring in two people. You get it. It's all about recruiting. Like any pyramid scheme, those who get in early get paid. The latecomers get fleeced. Just in case I haven't been clear: To participate in a pyramid scheme is a crime. Also consider that you may make money, but down the line a friend of a friend will be scammed. There are always many more victims than winners in pyramid schemes.

There's also the possibility that you could be charged with tax fraud or get a nasty tax bill with fines. Promoters of this scheme will tell you that the money you give is a gift and therefore the recipient isn't required to pay income taxes on the cash he or she receives. However, previous prosecutions of gifting-circle promoters prove otherwise. In one Connecticut case, two women were found guilty of tax fraud for running a gifting circle and not paying taxes on their gains. The ringleader was sentenced to 48 months in a federal prison.

Think about the logic behind the idea that the gift isn't taxable. If you are giving money as part of this scheme with the expectation that you will receive cash back, that's not a gift. You are giving with the expectation of receiving.

In tough times, it's understandable that people are duped and persuaded that this is a foolproof way to make money. You may be wondering how people could be so gullible.

Two kinds of people generally fall for a pyramid scheme. One group is just greedy. They see the opportunity to make fast money with little to no effort other than mining for recruits in their family and among their friends. The other group includes those who are in need. People who are struggling want to believe there's an easy way to make money.

The bottom line: This is not a legitimate way to build wealth.

I can't pay my mortgage. I saw an online ad for a company that says it can rescue me from a foreclosure. Is this legit?

It's shameful, but con artists cheer when a financial crisis hits. They know that people will be looking for a way to stay afloat, or, in the case of their home, to avoid a foreclosure. During the 2008 housing crisis, scammers promised homeowners they could help them get a mortgage modification, or they guaranteed that they could rescue them from a foreclosure. Many frantic homeowners fell victim to these scams because they had originally tried to contact their lender or loan servicer but had been volleyed around from one person to the next. Or they had to wait weeks for a response to their pleas for mortgage relief.

Typically, this is how a foreclosure scam works. A company will "guarantee" that it can stop a foreclosure, provide a mortgage modification, or negotiate to get you a better interest rate or reduce your monthly payment. The company may even appear to be government-sponsored or a nonprofit. The con: The company gets people to pay up-front fees, but after collecting their money, it does little, if anything, to assist them.

Don't believe the hype. Instead, to find legitimate foreclosure prevention assistance, get help from a nonprofit housing counseling group certified by the U.S. Department of Housing and Urban Development (HUD). You can find a HUD-approved housing counselor operating in your local community by calling 1-877-483-1515 or going to hud.gov. Click on the Resources tab and then on "HUD Approved Housing Counseling Agencies." A drop-down menu enables you to select your state, and from there you can find an agency.

If you see information about a foreclosure prevention company — online, by mail, by phone, or in an email — make sure it's HUD-approved *before* you do business with it. And don't take the company's word that it is certified by HUD. Go to hud.gov to double-check.

Most HUD-approved housing counselors provide no-cost or low-cost counseling services. If someone begins by charging you hundreds or thousands of dollars, walk away.

Additionally, if you are given a guarantee that the company can stop the foreclosure process, walk away. Because a lot of relief depends on what your lender or mortgage servicer will do, a legitimate counselor can't guarantee a certain result.

I know you don't want to lose your house. But I also don't want you to lose money you don't have by falling victim to a mortgage relief scam.

Is it okay to keep buying lottery tickets? Just one winning ticket will end all my financial problems.

I want you to stay hopeful. But you know that gambling isn't the way to fix your financial problems, right?

I could tell you not to buy a lottery ticket, but you probably still will, especially when jackpots get big. Instead, can we talk about the philosophy behind winning money to become financially stable? If you're playing often, I'm concerned about you. You may have developed a gambling addiction.

A survey by the Consumer Federation of America found that 38 percent of Americans with incomes under $25,000 said that winning the lottery was the most practical way for them to accumulate several hundred thousand dollars. It is not. But it's this kind of thinking—that there's a fast way to wealth—that makes you a target.

The moment someone tells me I can make easy money, I'm out.

Besides, research has shown that many lottery winners end up wasting their jackpot. Money easily gained is more easily lost. Why? Because if you can't manage the money you have now, then getting even more money won't make you better at financial stewardship.

I bought a time-share and now I can't afford the loan payments or maintenance fees. What are my options?

In good times, a time-share seems like a great idea. Lock in the price of nice vacations for the future in spacious condo-like accommodations. It's an easy sell, right?

But for many people, the time-shares they could once afford turn into a financial weight when the economy gets bad. Between the loan payments for the purchase and escalating maintenance fees, a time-share can be a real money pit. And the poolside daiquiri isn't enough to ease the pain.

But then you get a call from a company promising you relief. For a fee, it can get you out of your time-share contract. It's called the time-share exit business. Unfortunately, too often it's just a scam to take your money for little to no help.

What can you do?

Ask for relief. If you're having trouble making your time-share payments, contact the lender and see if you can get a forbearance until your financial situation improves. The company may provide a hardship exception if you still owe on the contract. You should also ask about refinancing if you can't handle the loan payments.

Sell. Timeshare Users Group, tug2.net, is a useful website for potential time-share owners, current owners, and those interested in selling their time-shares.

One important tip: Do not pay an up-front fee to a sales agent. Treat selling your time-share like you might selling a home. The agent gets paid when the sale is done. One reader wrote to me saying that she had paid $1,000 to two different companies promising to either sell or rent her time-shares. "Despite regular calls from me, they have never rented or sold either of the two time-shares we placed with them."

In one case, the Federal Trade Commission shut down a time-share resell company for falsely claiming that it had buyers or renters ready to buy or rent people's time-shares. The company charged owners up to $2,500 or more, but no sellers or renters were lined up. The FTC recouped about $2.7 million, resulting in refunds to more than 8,000 people. Unfortunately, the average check was for only $332. The company had bilked at least $15 million from time-share property owners, the FTC said.

If you're approached to sell your time-share, ask if the agent is licensed to sell real estate where your time-share is located. Verify the information with the state Real Estate Commission. Deal only with licensed real estate brokers and agents, and ask for references from satisfied clients. If you've purchased a time-share outside of the U.S., you'll need to research your options in that country. You may need to hire a local attorney to help you get out of the contract or give the time-share back.

One rule to remember in the time-share business is that it's not an investment. It is unlikely that you will get back anything near what you paid for the time-share.

Surrender. Many of the large time-share companies —
Marriott, Club Wyndham, Diamond Resorts — have exit programs in which the company will help you get out of your
time-share contract. But be careful not to be talked into up-
grading to get out of your current time-share and into another time-share contract.

Despite your pleas, the company may not listen or help you
get out of the time-share. But try anyway.

The American Resort Development Association (ARDA)
and the ARDA-Resort Owners Coalition (ARDA-ROC) say
that your first contact should be with your time-share resort
company. The organization has pulled together information
from companies offering exit help and a directory of advertis-
ing and resale providers, which can be found on responsible-
exit.com. On this site you'll find a checklist of items to take
care of if you are surrendering your time-share.

This tip does work. I received this testimony from one
person:

> *I own a time-share which has been paid off for about 10
> years, but I never use it. The maintenance fees go up ev-
> ery year and it's becoming harder to pay it along with
> the other debt I have. I decided to contact the time-share
> company and ask them if they would just take the time-
> share back because I couldn't pay the maintenance fees.
> I was shocked, they are taking it off my hands. So, I can
> now check this off my list.*

File for bankruptcy protection. If you've gotten behind
and you just can't pay this debt along with your other obligations, you may find that you need to file for bankruptcy. See
the FAQ on filing for Chapter 7 or Chapter 13.

For more information on time-shares, go to ftc.gov and search for "Timeshares and Vacation Plan" or consumer-fed.org and search for "Timeshare Scams and How to Avoid Them."

I keep getting calls saying that my Social Security number has been suspended. Can this happen?

I know it's scary to get one of these calls; I've gotten many myself. But they are without a doubt a scam.

Government impostor scams are growing and seem to increase during hard economic times. "Pretending to be the government may be scammers' favorite ruse," the FTC said in a blog post about top impostor scams. "Government impersonators can create a sense of urgent fear, telling you to send money right away or provide your Social Security number to avoid arrest or some other trouble."

The Social Security number scam is one that is particularly monstrous. It's terrifying if you're a senior living on Social Security and you get a call that claims your Social Security number has been blocked because it has been linked to a crime. The caller may threaten that the police are on the way. The crooks claim that your Social Security number has been suspended and that you need to pay a fee in order to "reactivate" it and avoid arrest. Or, the con artist demands that the victim buy gift cards and then instructs the person to give the caller the codes on the back of the cards. It's all a scam, every single word.

Someone from the Social Security Administration may call you if you're working with the agency on some issue or claim. But—and this is important—the agency won't just call you unexpectedly. Even if you have contacted Social Security about something, if you get a call back, hang up and call SSA's main number, 1-800-772-1213 (TTY 1-800-325-0778).

Most importantly, don't trust the number you see on your caller ID. Criminals are able to spoof numbers to make it appear that calls are from a government agency.

Please keep this in mind and pass it along to everyone you know, especially elderly relatives.

- Your Social Security number cannot be suspended, revoked, frozen, or blocked.
- A legitimate government employee will not ask you to wire money, send cash, or buy gift cards as a form of payment.
- If you are threatened with arrest or some other legal action, it's not the government calling.
- Never give out personal information such as your account numbers, passwords, Social Security number, mother's maiden name, or other identifying information.
- If you receive a call from someone asking for your Social Security number, bank account number, or credit card information, don't engage the caller. Instead hang up and report the call to the SSA's Office of the Inspector General. For more information, go to oig.ssa.gov/scam.

Really, this is about more than Social Security scams. So many imposter scams play on people's fear of negative government action.

Please do this for me:

- If you have elderly parents, put a note next to their phones to remind them about the scammer techniques. The Consumer Financial Protection Bureau has a free one-page information sheet in English and Spanish about Social Security scams. Go to consumerfinance. gov and search for "Social Security Scams." Be the go-to person for calls, emails, or text messages that friends and families aren't sure about. I am that person for my friends and relatives. I've made them promise to call me before responding to anything that looks sketchy. If you're not strong in this area, then identify someone in your life who can do this for you.

- Get the word out about caller ID. The technology has become so advanced these days that scammers can make the telephone number appear to be coming from your local area.
- If you're shopping or if you work for a retailer and see someone buying gift cards in huge amounts, ask some questions. Here's a short script to help you butt into their business: "Excuse me. I'm so sorry if this is intrusive, but I noticed you are buying a lot of gift cards. There are a lot of scams in which victims are told to buy gift cards. I'm just checking that you aren't being victimized." Then list the types of scams involving gift cards: Social Security number; relative is in trouble and needs bail money; you need to pay a tax bill; prize or sweepstakes.

Now is the time to be your brothers' and sisters' keeper.

Afterword

I started this book with the following statement: History has shown us that good financial times don't last forever. It's not a matter of if there will be another economic downturn, but when.

Hard times can fundamentally change a generation. The Great Depression caused such hardship, homelessness, and hunger that it created a nation of penny-pinchers. My grandmother, who appears throughout this book, was 15 when the Great Depression started and 25 when it ended.

The deprivation my grandmother experienced influenced just about every financial move she made. Throughout the rest of her life, Big Mama lived by the Depression-era mantra "Use it up, wear it out, make do, or do without."

Even as times got better, she feared the next recession. She believed she was always a paycheck away from poverty, even though she was an amazing saver. My grandmother despised debt because she worried it could lead to destitution when times got bad. Big Mama's extreme frugality and fear of not having enough never dissipated.

As I watched and, in many cases, helped people navigate the economic hardship of the COVID-19 pandemic, it became clear that the crisis should result in a generational shift, back to financial attitudes like those of survivors of the Great Depression.

Prior to the Great Depression, many Americans loathed the idea of receiving welfare. But President Franklin D. Roosevelt's New Deal programs, including the introduction of Social Security benefits, changed attitudes about government assistance.

And yet, as times got better, Americans returned to viewing people who needed government help as parasites. An American Enterprise Institute and *Los Angeles Times* poll in 2016 found that most Americans felt the government shouldn't bear the burden of helping the poor, a position that hadn't changed in three decades.

Then came the 2020 pandemic.

People demanded government assistance.

"The pandemic has laid bare deep inequalities as some groups in society have been disproportionately affected," a research consultant at Gallup wrote in March 2021. "Specifically, lower-income Americans, who are more likely to work in service jobs that have been affected by the pandemic, have suffered the greatest economic harm."

Three rounds of stimulus checks, along with monthly advance child-tax-credit payments, helped lift millions of families and millions of children out of poverty.

A 2021 poll by the Center for American Progress and GBAO Strategies found that American voters want the government to play a significant role in increasing the economic security of low-income families. An overwhelming majority of Americans favored an increase of direct rental and mortgage payment relief for families during crises such as the current coronavirus pandemic.

It's unfortunate that these changes in attitude aren't often followed by systemic long-term policy changes.

Americans are inconsistent about supporting struggling families. When there's an economic crisis, they step up. They back government aid policies during the heat of a crisis but just as quickly return to maxims like "pull yourself up by your bootstraps" when things begin to turn around. We must realize it takes more than a temporary change in attitude to defeat poverty or provide programs that help people support themselves.

As former *New York Times* columnist Nicholas Kristof wrote just as the pandemic hit the United States, "The bootstraps narrative often suggests that benefits programs are counterproductive because they foster 'dependency.' That may have been a plausible argument a generation ago, but the evidence now indicates that it is incorrect."

This narrative also implies that everyone is capable of helping themselves. This is not true. Some people need food or rental assistance. They need unemployment benefits when a crisis hits. "This is like arguing that because some people can run a four-minute mile, everyone can," Kristof wrote. "It's particularly hard for people to scramble up when they come from violent homes, poor schools or foster care, or face impediments of race or class. These can be challenges, but they can be addressed to some extent — but not by sermons about bootstraps."

During good times and bad, many families and individuals are left to rely on government relief systems, which are underfunded and overstressed.

The unemployment system, for example, was badly strained during the pandemic.

Here's what Pew Research Center says about unemployment benefits: "Despite some broad federal guidelines, claimants still face a hodgepodge of different state rules governing how they can qualify for benefits, how much they'll get, and how long they can collect them—because the United States does not have a single nationwide system for getting cash to jobless workers. Instead, it effectively has 53 separate systems run by the states (plus the District of Columbia, Puerto Rico, and the Virgin Islands), which are overseen but not controlled by the federal government."

And yet, the federal government relied heavily on the unemployment insurance system. But as Gallup reported, "Low-income, laid-off workers are less likely to be approved for unemployment insurance than high-income workers. When asked to describe their financial situation, the vast majority of laid-off, low-income workers are, at best, barely making ends meet. This raises questions about the efficacy of relief programs."

So, what does this mean for you as an individual?

Until policy changes catch up with the need, as best you can, you must think like my grandmother. Well, I don't mean you should be as fearful as she was, but follow her lead in practicing penny-pinching even after you've recovered from an economic crisis.

Don't forget the lessons of the pandemic. If you lived on less because you had to or because lockdowns forced you to, don't go back to living larger than you can afford. You can't count on a fickle American public and politicians to create a safety net when the next recession or economic downturn hits.

We'll get past the pandemic, but the COVID-19 crisis has

hopefully left you with a lasting memory of the need to live below your means – even when your means are more than enough.

Resources

Please note that this book is just your first step to receiving the information you need to manage your money during a crisis. The resources listed below are part of your next steps. I frequently recommend that people seek out the following organizations, nonprofits, consumer groups, and government agencies for more information.

I can't possibly answer all the questions you may have. I wish I could give you individual advice, but that isn't possible. But what I can do is provide you with sources I trust. This list includes websites I personally visit and consult on a regular basis. Most of them I have bookmarked on my computer.

This is by no means a complete list of every source you'll need to manage your money. And of course between the time I write this and the time you read it, websites and contact information might change.

CALCULATORS

Bankrate.com
This site has some of the most useful calculators you'll find online. Want to know how long it will take to pay off your

credit card if you make just the minimum payment every month? Go here. Need to figure out if you should refinance? Check out the refinance calculator.

NerdWallet.com
Go to nerdwallet.com/article/banking/savings-calculator for the savings calculator. In addition, you'll find many really good consumer-related articles at this site.

thepercentagechangecalculator.net
If you aren't sure how to calculate a percentage change or you want to double-check that you're actually getting that 30 percent off deal, use this online calculator.

WashingtonPost.com
I'm a bot. Search for "Michelle bot" to help you figure out how much you need to save for retirement.

CONSUMER ADVOCATES

Consumer Action
This nonprofit fights for your consumer rights and advocates for policies that encourage fairness in the marketplace. See consumer-action.org.

Consumer Federation of America
This is a research, advocacy, and education consumer group. See consumerfed.org.

Consumer Reports
In addition to product reviews, you'll find well-reported con-

sumer articles at consumerreports.com. If you can afford it, get a subscription to *Consumer Reports* magazine. It's well worth the money.

National Association of Unclaimed Property Administrators

This is an affiliate of the National Association of State Treasurers. At unclaimed.org you can search for unclaimed funds on databases maintained by each state.

National Community Reinvestment Coalition (NCRC)

This group fights discriminatory banking practices. See ncrc .org.

National Consumer Law Center (NCLC)

This group addresses the needs of low-income and elderly consumers. See consumerlaw.org.

National Consumers League

This nonprofit works to address the economic and social interests of consumers and workers. See nclnet.org.

National Housing Law Project

This group advocates for the rights of tenants and works to expand affordable housing options. See nhlp.org.

U.S. Public Interest Research Group (U.S. PIRG)

U.S. PIRG advocates for consumers on several issues, including bank fees and credit bureau abuses. See uspirg.org.

CREDIT BUREAUS/CREDIT REPORTING

Equifax
One of the three major credit bureaus. See equifax.com.

Experian
One of the three major credit bureaus. See experian.com.

TransUnion
One of the three major credit bureaus. See transunion.com.

Free Annual Credit Reports
This is the only official site to get your credit report from the three major credit bureaus, which you are entitled to receive every 12 months. You will need to provide your name, address, Social Security number, and date of birth to verify your identity. See annualcreditreport.com or call 1-877-322-8228.

CREDIT CARDS

CreditCards.com
Not only does this site help you compare credit card offers, but you'll also find articles and surveys that will help you use credit wisely.

WalletHub.com
A personal finance website with credit and credit card information and reports.

CREDIT SCORING

CreditKarma.com
You can get a free credit score.

Discover
Most lenders now offer consumers access to a free credit score. I like Discover's credit scorecard because of the way it lays out the five categories affecting your FICO score. This free credit score service offers specific explanations that can push you to credit-score perfection. See creditscorecard.com.

FICO
FICO is the company that created the most-used credit score. You can get your official credit score on myfico.com. You'll also find articles with a lot of information about how to improve your credit.

Freecreditscore.com
As part of Experian, you can get a free credit score.

DEBT MANAGEMENT/BUDGETING

The National Foundation for Credit Counseling
Go to nfcc.org for help with budgeting or get assistance with a debt management plan. Here you'll find a link to direct you to a nonprofit consumer credit counseling agency. You can also call 1-800-388-2227.

FRAUD

National Fraud Information Center/Internet Fraud Watch

During a financial crisis, scammers use the headline news to create new schemes. The site fraud.org will help you identify scams and/or file complaints about telemarketing and Internet fraud.

GOVERNMENT

Consumer Financial Protection Bureau (CFPB)

This watchdog federal agency was created to help consumers. See consumerfinance.gov.

Federal Deposit Insurance Corporation (FDIC)

This is the government agency charged with insuring your bank deposits. But the website, fdic.gov, has a number of consumer-related links to FDIC's Money Smart financial education program and economicInclusion.gov, which provides information on bank account ownership, use of prepaid cards, and nonbank financial transaction services.

Federal Reserve System

The information at federalreserve.gov can be a bit wonky, but the consumer finance surveys provide a lot of details on how Americans spend their money.

Federal Trade Commission (FTC)

Ftc.gov is my go-to website for many consumer issues. The FTC has an abundance of articles, tips, and blog posts that can help you with issues involving your debit or credit card or alert you to the latest scams.

Internal Revenue Service

I know what you may be thinking. Why would you go to the IRS website, irs.gov, if you don't owe the government any money? But the site has a lot of answers to your tax questions. Not sure about deductions? Go here. Set up an account so you can check your tax payment history or your refund status. I'm on this site all the time checking for the latest tax news.

National Association of Unclaimed Property Administrators

You can search for unclaimed property and cash at unclaimed .org.

Office of the Comptroller of the Currency (OCC)

You can find answers to questions regarding national banks and federal savings associations at HelpWithMyBank.gov.

USA.gov

The Consumer Issues link on USA.gov is a guide for consumers to learn scam types, state or local fraud protection resources, and pathways for action if a qualifying consumer problem occurs. You'll also find a link to State Consumer Protection Offices (usa.gov/state-consumer).

U.S. Department of Housing and Urban Development (HUD)

Go to hud.gov to find a HUD-approved housing counseling agency if you need help when you can't pay your mortgage.

U.S. Justice Department
Check justice.gov for updates on consumer fraud.

LEGAL SERVICES

ImmigrationLawHelp.org
This is an online directory of free or low-cost nonprofit immigration legal services.

Legal Services Corporation (LSC)
You'll find help locating legal aid services at lsc.gov.

National Disability Rights Network
At ndrn.org you'll find legal service providers by state for people with disabilities.

Nolo.com
This website has a wealth of information about legal matters, from filing for bankruptcy protection to advice on how to handle debt collectors.

StatesideLegal.org
This site specifically serves veterans, military members, and their families.

U.S. Department of Veterans Affairs
At va.gov you'll find a list of legal service clinics; search for "legal help."

Upsolve

This nonprofit provides a free app that helps low-income families file for bankruptcy for free. It's best to get an attorney, but if you can't find free legal help or afford representation, this tool can walk you through filing for bankruptcy. See upsolve.org.

OLDER ADULTS

AARP

You may view this organization as a way to get senior discounts, but it's much more than that. On the site, aarp.org, are excellent articles and tips to help seniors during a crisis.

Eldercare Locator

Find local offices on aging and legal services organizations for older adults and their families at eldercare.acl.gov. You can also call 1-800-677-1116.

National Council on Aging (NCOA)

NCOA says that one in three older adults is economically insecure. This organization provides information to help older adults manage their money. See ncoa.org.

RETIREMENT

Pension Rights Center

This consumer organization is dedicated to protecting and promoting the retirement security of American workers. See pensionrights.org.

Social Security Administration (SSA)

You may think the only time you might visit ssa.org is when you are ready to file to get your Social Security benefit. But you should be going there regularly for information about retirement, including setting up a *my* Social Security account. You want to make sure you create an account so you can get your statement to review the estimate of future Social Security benefits, among other things.

FINANCIAL INFORMATION WEBSITES

Bankrate.com

I visit this site at least several times a week.

Investopedia.com

You'll find answers to questions about personal finance, investing, and retirement.

NerdWallet.com

I find some of the most helpful and accessible personal finance articles on this site.

Fool.com

When you visit this site, for Motley Fool, click on the link for Personal Finance.

FINANCIAL NEWS SITES

Kiplinger.com

Honestly, when I want to be sure I've got something right, especially about retirement, I head right over to this site.

NewYorkTimes.com

You'll find some of my favorite personal finance writers and columnists at the *Times*. Sure, it is a competitor to my employer, but I would be petty not to recommend that you read its reporting too.

USAToday.com

I love *USA Today*'s money section. Its coverage is spot on and its articles are very accessible.

WashingtonPost.com

Yes, I work for the *Post*, but that also means I know how hard the business section staff works to bring people the most up-to-date economic and personal financial news.

Your local newspaper

I know you don't want to pay for a subscription. But to manage your money better, especially during a financial crisis, you need to be informed. The best way to do this with news you can trust is to read the business section of your local newspaper.

Acknowledgments

No effort like this is ever completed without the help of a multitude of people. I want to thank Rick Wolff, former senior executive editor at HMH Books and Media. Rick, you reached out with a simple mission of providing a guiding light to people in need of advice during a pandemic that cost so many lives and left millions unemployed and worried about their financial security. Thank you for selecting me for this endeavor, and thanks to the entire team at Houghton Mifflin Harcourt for believing in me and for taking on this project. Special thanks to Deb Brody, Emma Peters, Jenny Freilach, and Liz Duvall, who is a rock star of a copyeditor.

To my agent, Richard Abate, and the staff at 3 Arts Entertainment, I'm so appreciative of your continued representation, which has helped expand my reach.

I'm so incredibly blessed to have a wonderful group of friends and neighbors, who have provided encouragement throughout my career, including Alexa Steele, Andrea Moore, Sade Olufemi Dennis, and Wiley Hall. Thank you to my 8@8 couples' group — Larry and Terri Ames, Patrick and Deborah Berry, Malcolm and Barbara Streeter. To my Prosperity Partners Ministry leadership and curriculum team at First Baptist Church of Glenarden, thank you for having my back and for working so tirelessly to help run a financial program that assists so many people to become better money managers. I'm grateful for the service of the couples who assist in the marriage and money class my husband and I teach: Karrie and Audrey Butler, Cleveland and LaShaun Kelly, Leonard and Margaret Butler. There are so many at my church who help center me and keep my focus on the things that really matter, including Reverends Skip and Beverly Little and the FBCG Couples Ministry.

To my Color Me Read Book Club: no, you don't have to read this book, but I appreciate your celebration of my work. Always. We have become a family whom I adore and treasure.

To my editors and colleagues at the *Washington Post,* thank you for your support. Thank you, Suzanne Goldenberg, Sophie Yarborough, and Daniel de Visé for helping me become a better writer and for seeing me and believing in my mission and vision to provide the financial guidance that people need to find financial peace.

Finally, to my family members, who didn't fuss when after yet another telephone call I said, "Can't talk, I'm working on the book." Love you much, Monique, Matwia, Michael, Kim, LaPorcha, Tom, Monica, Lauren, Ronnie, Jordan, Lois, and Courtney. I appreciate you, LaQuasha and Daryan, for your willingness to listen to an aunt who is always in your business. I'm so proud of how you are managing your finances. To my children—Olivia, Kevin, and Jillian—I know you've had to put up with a lot of money lessons and lectures. You let me practice on you, albeit unwittingly. Above all, I'm so proud of your kind and loving spirits. I also must give a special shout-out to Jillian, who assisted me on the book.

And then there is my husband, Kevin, who is an amazing

editor who after his workday read over every section of the book, offering input that was invaluable. Every spouse deserves a partner like you — loving, patient, constructively critical when needed, and always supportive. I could not do any of what I do without you. I love you to the moon and back!

About the Author

MICHELLE SINGLETARY is a personal finance columnist for the *Washington Post*. Her award-winning column, The Color of Money, is syndicated by the Washington Post News Service & Syndicate. She was the financial expert for *The Revolution*, a daytime program on ABC. She also hosted her own national television program, *Singletary Says*, on TV One. She is a frequent contributor to various NPR programs and has appeared on national talk shows and television networks, including CNN, NBC's *Today*, and *The Early Show on CBS*. In her spare time she is the director of a financial ministry she founded at her church. As part of this ministry, she and her husband volunteer to teach financial literacy to prison inmates. She is a graduate of the University of Maryland at College Park. She received the *Washington Post*'s prestigious Eugene Meyer Award. She was also given a Distinguished Alumni Award from Johns Hopkins University, where she earned a master's degree in business and management. She lives in Maryland with her husband and three children.